How to Sell

How ·to· Sell

SUCCEEDING IN A NOBLE PROFESSION

THE COMPLETE GUIDE TO PROSPECTING, SELLING, AND NEGOTIATING TO WIN

CHARLES FELLINGHAM
AND ANDRE O'BRIEN

New York

How to Sell
Succeeding In A Noble Profession
The Complete Guide To Prospecting, Selling, And Negotiating To Win

Published in New York, New York, by Morgan James Publishing. Morgan James and The Entrepreneurial Publisher are trademarks of Morgan James, LLC.
www.MorganJamesPublishing.com

The Morgan James Speakers Group can bring authors to your live event. For more information or to book an event visit The Morgan James Speakers Group at www.TheMorganJamesSpeakersGroup.com.

ISBN 978-1-63047-829-2 paperback
ISBN 978-1-63047-831-5 eBook
ISBN 978-1-63047-830-8 hardcover
Library of Congress Control Number: 2015916628

Cover Design by:
Chris Treccani
www.3dogdesign.net

Interior Design by:
Bonnie Bushman
The Whole Caboodle Graphic Design

Table of Contents

Introduction

"Every person has a longing to be significant; to make a contribution; to be a part of something noble and purposeful."

—John C. Maxwell [1]

Sales is a noble profession; really? Unfortunately, popular public opinion would disagree with this statement as evidenced by the following sign placed outside a neighborhood business; "we shoot every third salesman, and the second one just left." No doubt salespeople may be viewed this way, that is, until one meets a true professional. Fortunately, the professional salespeople that we train and coach shatter this negative perception.

"When you are able to shift your inner awareness to how you are able to serve others, and when you make this the central focus of

your life, you will then be in a position to know true miracles in your progress towards prosperity"

— Wayne Dyer[2]

Every day, we witness professional sales men and women work tirelessly in an effort to connect with their customers. They desire to convert a stranger into a friend and help that friend solve a challenge, sometimes the customer is unaware even exists. Once the issue is resolved, the new friend is better off and ready to embark on a relationship that will continue to result in mutual reward. What is more noble and purposeful than living a life of service to others?

"There is nothing noble in being superior to your fellow men. True nobility lies in being superior to your former self."

— Ernest Hemingway[3]

True professionals value the effort necessary for self-improvement. It's an endeavor driven by a constant need to heighten one's skills so they can more effectively serve the customer. They strive to see the world from the perspective of their customer. This perspective helps them to collect information about their customers' needs, synthesize it into useful plans and present solutions that will be easily instituted by the customer. What is nobler than investing one's time, without fanfare, in an effort to add value to the lives of strangers?

"We should be too big to take offense and too noble to give it."

— Abraham Lincoln[4]

Professionals do not take offense when engaging a potential/current customer. When a prospect says that they are not interested in speaking with the pro, either by word or deed, the professional understands that it is their responsibility to make a favorable first impression, build rapport and develop the mutual interest in the conversation. This role is not for the "faint at heart", because rejection sometimes is delivered swiftly and often. The opposite is equally true. The professional will use every skill they possess to help the customer feel better as a result of this interaction.

The salesperson realizes that when they execute their role professionally, the customer will feel strengthened, enlightened, and satisfied as a result. Never, never, never should the customer feel like they have lost something during the engagement. There is nobility in striving to leave someone feeling better as a result of an encounter with you.

Sales is absolutely a noble profession. The actions necessary to be considered a professional salesperson ignites organizations to achieve and grow, brings ideas to reality which drives innovation and creates personal bonds that often last a lifetime. During our sales activities we are exhibiting the finest of human values and we provide countless benefits to our customers. In our own small way, the results we create are changing lives, changing businesses and changing the world and these changes will live on long after we are gone. Scottish novelist, Muriel

Spark, wrote, *"When a noble life has prepared old age, it is not decline that it reveals, but the first days of immortality".*[5]

Preface

What makes sales professionals successful? What gives them the ability to earn substantial incomes? We will answer these questions while giving you the road map to become one of them. Whether you're a sales professional or amateur, an entrepreneur or sales manager, it's time to smile. You have arrived at a serendipitous event, where preparedness and timing have collided with your desire to improve your skills, creating the opportunity for you to realize your goal of becoming a top sales professional.

We are professional business people and sales trainers that have dedicated many years of our lives to helping sales professionals and their leaders go beyond just getting better at what they do. We help people like you achieve breakthroughs in your professional career. A breakthrough happens when we grow past our present state. We do something different and better, in such a way as to create an outstanding result. Let's just say that a breakthrough is our ability to take a giant leap in our capability to the point where we are doing something different in order to achieve a better result. We assist participants in our workshops to create breakthroughs for themselves in the transfer and application of sales behaviors and skills. We expect this book will help you do the same.

An acquaintance that played minor league baseball for the Atlanta Braves baseball farm system, once discussed a coach that worked with him in college to improve his hitting. He had a breakthrough moment during one session and when the ball was pitched, he realized that for the first time, he saw very clearly the spin of the ball. He said, "...it was as though I could see the ball hurling toward me in slow motion and I crushed it. I was a significantly better hitter at that moment and that breakthrough propelled me forward like no other!"

We want to propel you into the next level of your career and the methods used in this book are all designed to spur breakthroughs in every aspect of your sales skills. We have helped timid communicators evolve into fearless closers and inexperienced presenters have grown into platform professionals.

This book follows the path that professional trainers use to effectively transfer training from the training room to the marketplace. The twelve principles are applicable throughout the sales processes. The sales, prospecting and negotiation processes are time tested and proven.

We designed this book exclusively for you because we are rewarded by your success.

Acknowledgements

The most difficult part of this book to write, was the acknowledgements. There are so many people who played a role in making this book a reality. We are so incredibly fortunate to have so many wonderful friends and we admittedly are concerned that if we try to list them all, we may leave someone out. Instead, we would like to say, thanks so much to our many supporters (you know who you are). We do have a few friends who deserve special mention:

A very special thank you to the incredibly professional team at Morgan James Publishing, your support was deeply appreciated.

Cathi Rodgers, Alicia Randolph and Andy Greider, thank you for taking the time to render editing assistance with the book. Your selfless efforts are truly appreciated. And to the folks that inspired us…

Tom and Mollie Breazeale, Ercell Charles – the reason we train professionals
Jim Olson—mastery at telling business stories
Vernon Roberts, Bill Spenla—inspiration for making your vision a reality
Janet Logan—the most creative training executive I know
Carol Roby—the Carol in the 1st chapter was you
Glenn Leonardi—A savy legal mind with exceptional leadership skill
Bill Rathbun—the greatest sales manager I have ever known
Pierre Jambon—role model for our charisma section
Arlen Moulder—taught me to be consistently reliable
Wendy Johnson—inspirational leader that never gives up
Ron Eishelman—perhaps the greatest salesman that ever lived
Janet McCormick—the most engaged L&D person I have ever known
Bob Littell—the most unselfish person on the planet
John Petraborg—our role model for principle one
Marianne Dougherty—every person counts, every moment counts

CHAPTER 1
Mind vs. Muscle

Everything starts with our attitude. It is the inner game that sets the great sales professionals apart from the good ones. By 'inner game' we mean the attitude required to push past verbal obstacles, criticism and complaints. It is the mental state that overcomes rejection and barriers to our deals from inside or outside of our own organization. The inner game drives our efforts to a successful outcome, drawing upon innate instinct and skill. A strong attitude presses us to write the winning email, create follow through plans, prepare the presentations, schedule and conduct meetings with winning results, even if the client has decades more industry experience than us. And our attitude presses us to develop the will to do all of these things at an accelerated pace.

Attitude is in a class by itself. We cannot simply call it an emotion or feeling. Attitude goes beyond that. It is underpinned by the deepest beliefs we have about our self and our world. It is the thing that changes the world and relentlessly strives for more and better. Without a positive winning attitude, we drift. With it, we drive. It allows us to balance competitiveness with cooperation and gives us a strong will to win, and simultaneously evokes patience, enough to wait for the winning moment.

Salespeople worth their salt are expected to execute the basics well. We call this selling "muscle". Yes, we are expected to be outgoing, likable, self-motivated people with good communication and organizational skills. We are experienced coaches and can easily predict the dimly lit future of those aspiring salespeople lacking muscle and confidence in fundamental sales skills. Be assured, that challenges can be overcome and your capabilities can be strengthened with developmental skills training. Our training helps you build selling muscle every day. Visit www.salesuniverse.com for additional information on our virtual workshops and video series.

The process part of this book is designed to build selling muscle. Yet without the right attitude, we cannot expect any training to stick, nor would we expect the salesperson to have a successful longstanding career in this challenging profession.

To quote a sales coach from our past, "You won't deliver your 'A' game until you understand your 'Y' game." By this, we mean that we need to know what we want to gain from our efforts in the sales game. What is in it for us? This is the inner game that provides the juice for our progress.

Maybe your "Y" is monetary gain. You may be more excited about achieving a goal or conquering a challenge. The attitude that says, "don't give me the tee shirt or trophy; just give me another challenge to conquer!" Many of us are absolutely jazzed by simply helping others solve problems or, maybe it's the relationships with clients and industry peers that matters most to you. And there are those of us that visualize the sales role as a stepping-stone to executive management. If there was ever a time when we must be comfortable with our own motivations, this is it. Our ability to focus on our "Y" will be very helpful during the difficult moments that are sure to present themselves in our profession.

We must be self-motivated. The first thing on our to-do list in the morning should be to focus on creating a positive attitude for the day. Something as simple as a quote or phrase that becomes a mantra that can carry us through the day is an excellent practice. We have witnessed salespeople have great success by putting a symbol of monetary or a physical reward in a visible place in their work or living space. It could be monopoly money or a picture of a desired automobile, some have even created an entire "vision notebook" with affirmations and pictures of their new life. Whatever direction you choose, we highly recommend the daily exercise of taking a moment to visualize yourself enjoying the fruits of your success as though you have already attained your desired outcome.

Can we develop and maintain this inner strength and ineffable attitude, or do we need to be born with this ability? Certainly those born into situations where they already had a natural persuasive ability and enjoyed the support and nurturing of gregarious parents or relatives who served as strong role models would have an advantage. But we are not in competition with them, only ourselves. So we must set out by doing the work to strengthen our attitude as a first act. We are not trying to overcome pre-adult inhibitions or deficiencies, but rather build on the strengths we possess now. At our most fundamental state, we must have faith in ourselves and our abilities. Many successful professionals came from lessor beginnings and a thicket of obstacles, only to overcome them on the road to their success. They did, so can you. There are no excuses for us, only inspiration to drive beyond our self-assigned deficiencies.

William Hutchison Murray was a Scottish mountaineer and writer. He wrote the following passage in his book, *The Scottish – Himalayan Expedition*, while spending 3 years in a German prisoner of war camp during WW II:

> *"Until one is committed, there is hesitancy, the chance to draw back, always ineffectiveness. Concerning all acts of initiative (and creation), there is one elementary truth that ignorance of which kills countless ideas and splendid plans: that the moment one definitely commits oneself, then Providence moves too. All sorts of things occur to help one that would never otherwise have occurred. A whole stream of events issues from the decision, raising in one's favor all manner of unforeseen incidents and meetings and material assistance, which no man could have dreamed would have come his way. Whatever you can do, or dream you can do, begin it. Boldness has genius, power, and magic in it. Begin it now."*

Success in this profession is birthed in a great love affair. Fall in love with yourself and your ability to perform. Everyone benefits when you allow yourself to genuinely love the idea of working with people and doing all you can to help them solve their problems. Daily recognize your love for your company, its products and the ability you have to add value to the lives of others.

Being in sales requires an attitude that supports a love for the profession. During a Saturday morning workshop for commission salespeople called "Warming up to the Cold Call", Adam, an aspiring sales professional at only 16 years of age, entered the room and filled the space with his personal energy. He spent the first few hours of the workshop sitting on the edge of his seat, leaning forward and clinging to every word. When given the opportunity, he expressed that he was there because he wanted to learn more about selling. He said that he had always wanted to be in sales and always will be. He had a paper route with his older brother and was an award winning subscription sales leader in his territory. His attitude and passion for the subject was contagious. At the end of the workshop, seasoned sales professionals spoke with him, giving him encouragement while also feeding on his energy and enthusiasm for the subject. In a way, this young man reaffirmed to the other professionals in the room "Y" they were in the profession. We can always tell when we are in the presence of someone who has that type of commitment and enthusiasm for the proud profession we are in, because their energy is electrifying.

Maintaining a positive outlook and attitude is our challenge. We have endeavored to give you a way to sustain it while keeping a keen eye on the best behaviors which will predict a high level of success. Our twelve principles of selling can become your anchor and can be used together or separately in the right moments to accelerate your results.

The "Law of Attraction"[6], states that the energy that we put out in the universe comes back to us, be it positive or negative. How do we apply the Law to Sales? We must diligently engage with the expectation of success for our customers and ourselves to support the law. We are constantly playing the inside game of sales, which involves visualizing the steps necessary to move people in our pipeline from prospect to customer. Winning at this game requires a higher level of energy and intention. We must act on our inner drives, feelings and desires. This outward action creates a universal reaction. Since the law of attraction suggests equivalence between energy expended and energy received.

When we leave our home to go to our office or a client meeting, it is "game on," and time to perform. We must engage at "performance level", just as an actor would engage when the curtain goes up. It's time to be genuine, natural, relaxed and confident. Be authentic, but remember we are performers. Performers operate at a different level of energy than most of us. Our customers are looking to us to lead conversations, open meetings, tell stories and offer advice. They also expect us to be active listeners and demonstrate genuine interest in what they are saying. So when we engage our prospects and customers, remember; "lights, camera, action!"

CHAPTER 2

The Twelve Principles of Selling

Sales is human nature amplified. Let's face it, when we are engaged in selling, we are communicating, understanding and being persuasive at the highest possible level. We are intentionally fostering and sustaining relationships with people or groups. Planned acts of kindness and providing goodwill are the norm. While we are expecting something in return for all of this goodness, we are genuine and sincere in its delivery. We made it a practice to call buyers when their favorite sports team won and we forwarded unsolicited articles to prospects because we knew they would value its content. We might only do these things for our best friends, yet top salespeople conduct themselves this way as a standard. What makes the sales profession so noble is that the top salespeople exhibit the best human values consistently.

Carol is one of the most successful sales professionals I know. She works out of an office in New York but sells her company's services throughout North America. I can confidently say that she exhibits the best human values. She is reliable, honest, open, positive, cheerful, credible and unselfish. From day one, she made me feel more like a friend than a business colleague. I believe she is so successful because she stays true to her own values that are communicated, outwardly, to her clients. When we are transparent as communicators, those close to us know what we believe and feel because we are able to authentically communicate our deepest truths in ways beyond just words. We need to be fully aware that our feelings and beliefs do signal our listeners. Carol is able to build trust in her relationships by living the way she does, which comes naturally to her, so her clients feel she is entirely genuine.

So what are the best human values? You know them. Think of what they are and write them out. To get you started, here are a few; be honest, be reliable, be kind, empathetic and helpful to others… you see where we are going with this. So, we in sales are doing these things all the time at a high level. This is why sales is such a noble profession.

Through the years, we have discovered that living a life based on sound principles gives us focus and creates a clear path for consistent behaviors that have benefited us enormously in our business relationships. They are a kind of reliable fuel that powers our behaviors. We have fed on principles from some of the best sources, Dale Carnegie's 9 principles[7] for becoming a friendlier person and Stephen Covey's *7 Habits of Highly Effective People*[8] (which were really principles), just to name a few. So we developed our list of principles for professionals to live and embody. The 12 principles of selling are a result of conversations with thousands of salespeople from over a combined 35 years of sales training workshops and combined 50 years of selling success.

The 12 Principles of Selling

1. **Stay enthused and passionate, always**
2. **Rejection is a state of mind; conquer it**
3. **Be Charismatic**
4. **Build your personal brand**
5. **Be Naturally Curious**
6. **Every Moment Counts, be in the moment**
7. **Every person counts, let them know**
8. **Manage your time**
9. **Manage your relationships**
10. **Take care of your customer**
11. **Know your products**
12. **Know your competition**

Principle 1: Stay enthused and passionate, always

We have ranked this principle number one for good reason. Simply put, we sell ourselves first, then our company and then our products or services. Should you be lucky enough to have people immediately say that you are consistently passionate and enthusiastic, you will win most of the battles you face in life and be more successful in making first impressions and selling yourself. It will also enable you to make friends easily and you can expect to be offered leadership roles throughout your life. It is the strongest of personal brand traits and why we feel it is so important to adopt as part of the formula for personal success.

Being consistently enthusiastic and passionate requires intentional fortitude. You need to wake up in the morning with a positive outlook and endeavor to sustain it throughout every day. Owning this principle will enable you to perform the other eleven principles with greater ease. It will enable you to have an optimistic outlook which permits clear communication and stronger relationships. There is a physiology component involved with enthusiasm and passion. We don't know whether the endorphins and adrenalin are released first and we then feel and exhibit the euphoria, or whether we experience or manufacture enthusiasm and our body's chemical reaction follows. Let's just assume that they happen simultaneously and that we can create it through intentional mental process.

There is an old story of a wealthy man with twin sons. One son was an optimist, the other, a pessimist. The father was convinced that his sons needed more balance in their lives so he decided on very unique gifts for their birthday. For his pessimist son, he purchased a $5000 top-of-the-line road bicycle and placed it in his room. For his optimist son, he had a truck full of horse manure placed in his playroom. The father visited his pessimist son expecting to see a vibrant, excited 12 year-old. Instead he was shocked to see his son's reaction. His pessimist son was very upset.

He shouted, "Father, I thought you loved me? How could you do this to me? Do you know what this is; it's a top-of-the-line road bike. I can't ride this. If I ride it, someone will surely punch me in the nose and take it from me. If I do make it to school on this bike, all the kids will hate me because I will look like a show off. Oh, what a horrible birthday!"

The father understood that he missed the mark with that son, so he went to check on his optimist son. He figured there was no way this son could be happy with his gift. When he arrived at the playroom, he heard hysterical laughter from inside. He opened the door to find his son sitting in middle of the pile of manure laughing, playing and throwing the manure all around the room. He asked his son, why he was so happy. His son shouted, "thank you so much daddy, I love you!!! This is wonderful, I could not be happier. With all of this manure, there must be a pony here somewhere!!!"

This joke is well over 100 years old and it has changed much over the years, but the message has remained the same. We do not see the world as it is; we see the world as we are. The sales profession is not for the faint of heart. It can be a very difficult job and we must be diligent when managing our attitude daily so we can always engage our world with enthusiasm and passion.

Our sales activities are really a series of communications through various means. The objective of this communication is to match client needs to our solution. To convince a client, we always need to make a logical argument. To move a client to take action, we need to make the emotional appeal. Both logic and emotion work in tandem and are essential to all decisions and actions. The word "emotion" has its own Wiki page that highlights its essence and primal origin at the brain stem, the "ancient" part of our brain. The word is derived from Greek, and literally means, "move to action." Influencing our client to have a positive emotional response is a necessary element to gain their trust and complete the sales process.

Do you want to put a sense of urgency in your clients' actions? Passion becomes the catalyst for that result and an important part of any communication. We must have passion for our company, products, services, our colleagues, our clients and ourselves. We cannot give what we do not have. We are transparent as communicators and our clients know our belief level because we demonstrate it loud and clear through our words and actions. Here is an easy exercise to help you maintain your enthusiasm when needed:

- STEP 1 — Make a list of every activity and experience that makes you smile and consequently helps you "feel great". For example, listening to music, spending time with specific family members, thinking about your last sales win, hitting golf balls, praying, exercising. Make the list as long as possible and keep adding to it as new experiences qualify. This is List A

- STEP 2 — Review the list and separate those activities easily engaged in during the day, when a boost in enthusiasm is needed. This is List B
- STEP 3 — Stay intentional about managing your attitude. When needed, review both list and engage in the most appropriate activities that will result in a positive change in your state of mind.

Enthusiasm is the expression of passion. This is the first lesson for the professional salesperson. We must get passionate about our company, its products and services, and the people with whom we are communicating. Only then can our passion be successfully transferred to others. It is this passion that can influence the emotional response from our customer to move the selling process forward.

Principle 2: Rejection is a state of mind; conquer it

I (Charles) have always loved the winning and losing aspect of selling. The situations that I competed in were high dollar, big- volume- needle-movers. The wins meant expansion of our capacity and the losses meant jobs were lost. Many of the contracts were multi-million dollars, multi-year deals with multi-year sales cycles. I won many and lost a few. Occasionally, losing a deal is one of those inevitable things that happen when you are in sales. The losses were hard to take and required some attitude adjustment on my part. The mental process to accept a loss and move on involves an intentional act to spend time to learn from the loss and incorporate that lesson learned into future campaigns.

It is easy to fall into an emotional hole after a loss, or especially after a series of them. An effective way of coping with these feelings is to adopt the attitude of an optimist and look for opportunities to convert failures into successes. Remain optimistic. Optimists have better health, longer life spans, better relationships and more fun. Optimists expect to win and when they do, they build from it. And, even though they don't expect to lose, they learn from every loss. Losses are just another reason to learn more and better ways to win again. Optimists turn a loss into a 'lessons learned exercise' which creates a winning event for them. They know that the best result that can come from a loss is the awareness of the mistakes that contributed to it, so they may be avoided in the future.

A sales rep shared a story where he acquired a multimillion, multi-year account in 1998. The business was lost to his main competitor in 2008 at the end of the 10-year contract. The account is a well-known company in the package delivery space whose main corporate value was on-time delivery. The business was lost due to price and service deficiencies, which was not unique to those who deliver this type of service. When it was lost he set about to win it back. He forged a long term, campaign mentality and maintained his contacts with consistent touch points. The business was won five years later. And the rep was viewed as a hero by his own leadership for the win. He employed the art of using a loss as a motivation for the next win, to near perfection.

In our negotiation workshops we teach that winning means having leverage. Part of having leverage is having an adequate alternative to a deal settlement. Having a healthy inventory of sales opportunities that can convert to a sale (your prospect pipeline) is crucial to conquering loss and remaining optimistic. Having a healthy prospect pipeline facilitates your leverage. It also means that there are more wins in the pipeline ready to deliver which takes the sting out of losses. Hope is a great motivator. We hope we meet or exceed our goal and hope that we can work hard and find success in our career. But hope can also be defined as "delayed disappointment." Have you heard the cliché "hope is not a plan", well it isn't and to avoid disappointment we must act to convert hope to our reality. This means we should position ourselves for the next win by keeping in mind that within our pipeline are real 'closable' opportunities waiting in the wings.

To have a winning attitude also means having a sense of urgency for success. It is not something that we want to outwardly show because we certainly don't want to appear desperate. This is more about an internal drive. During a sales workshop for commission-only salespeople, one of the participants shared the following compelling story. He sold jewelry at a store that specialized in wedding and engagement rings. He had worked at this particular jewelry store for almost five weeks without having made a significant sale. His wife told him to stay there, sleep there if necessary and not to come home until he made a sale. Thank goodness for his wife and his willingness to take her advice. True to form, he made two large sales the next day. For him, necessity was the seed of motivation, creativity, and production.

We should prepare ourselves for every eventuality by mentally practicing 'what if' scenarios. While it is good to be enthusiastic, it is also prudent to have real expectations about potential outcomes. This is our opportunity to effectively manage our pipeline and keep our organization aware of the real possibility of wins and losses. This keeps it real and can help to reduce some of the stress which results from repeated rejection and losses.

Our ability to overcome losses is an integral part of our success. It requires us to be real with its possibility without letting the opportunity of a negative outcome dilute our attitude. Highly effective sales professionals learn from losses while positioning themselves for the next success.

Principle 3: Be Charismatic

Charisma is that innate quality in a person that seems to have its own gravitational pull. When charisma is used for good, it can do a lot of heavy lifting when we are trying to sell our ideas or gain the collaboration of others. But what is this elusive quality? After observing people who possess true personal charisma, we have come to understand two things:

- Everyone has charisma
- Charisma comes from our ability to focus on other people

Simply stated, personal charisma is your ability to make the other person feel good about themselves in your presence.

When you acknowledge others before yourself, people take mental notice. And, it positively reflects well on both you and them. This is the draw that makes people want to be part of your expanding network of friends and colleagues.

An executive was well known for making his team feel important and valued. When he introduced a team member to someone, he would comment about a positive trait or a strength the person possessed. It ignited the conversation that followed and had a lasting impact on the leader's brand image. We refer to this action as a 'spotlight' comment. Likewise, the same executive had a unique way of acknowledging the strengths and actions of his team and would lavish praise when deserved. We call this action a 'floodlight' comment. While his steady unselfish use of spotlight and floodlight commenting took the attention away from him, it came back to him in the form of respect and admiration. Most everyone that knew him would say that he had charisma, and it was his unselfish attention to others that created this label.

The question many ask during our workshops is, "Does everyone have charisma or is reserved for a lucky few who were born with it?" The answer is always, "Everyone has it, but most of us repress it because we don't know how to harness its power." Most of us are unaware that we even have charisma. But now knowing that we do, we just need to know how to set it free. You have full permission to release it and enjoy its effect on your ability to be confident and persuasive. Now let's discuss how it is done.

Here are tips for building your personal charisma.

1. Remember names, use them, and build relationships.

During a coaching workshop with five managers of a major big-box retail chain, each was asked to set a personal leadership goal to improve their relationship with their teams. They were asked to report on their progress over the period of 10 weeks. In preparation for this exercise, one of the managers was asked if he knew the names of his employees. He responded, "Please realize that there are over 300 employees and with turnover, knowing their names seems impossible." He was then asked, what would be the result to walk through the halls at any time of day and greet associates by name? The positive visual of that idea motivated the manager to commit to making it happen. Over the next few weeks of his coaching sessions his transformation was remarkable. He said that not only did he learn the 300 names but he also developed strong relationships with many. As he walked down the hall greeting his associates, they enthusiastically greeted him back. His personal brand evolved from an aloof manager to a charismatic leader. His workers began to open up to him. From those relationships, he learned about the true inner workings of the store… the good and the bad. He was now able to solve problems and create strategic initiatives with willing associates beside him. The simple act of committing to learning names became the catalyst to a more effective management style which affected both his professional and personal life in a big way.

This example is an excellent illustration of building relationships by learning, remembering and using names. The two keys to remembering someone's name sounds simple and they are, but they are rarely employed. First, we must change our inner voice. So many of us have convinced ourselves that we can't remember names. We say this repeatedly to others and ourselves — "Oh, I am bad at remembering names." Sound familiar? It is time to change the script and admit we are getting better every day at remembering names. Second, we simply must make the decision to remember the name. It takes some effort from most of us to commit a name to memory and we must be willing to do the work. Once you have decided to remember the name, try some of the following techniques:

- Use the name immediately during the conversation.
- Repeat the name to yourself.
- Take the first opportunity to write it down. Add a short story about the person – include where you met, what you discussed and anything unique, different or interesting about the conversation.
- Clarify the spelling, pronunciation or meaning of the name. Any discussion about their name will help you remember it.
- Find an association with the name that will help you remember it.
- Does it rhyme with something familiar? Is his name David Hankey like "Hankey Pankey"?
- Examine their face for some characteristic you can relate to their name. Do they have brilliantly white teeth and is their name Sarah Shine?
- Is their occupation helpful in your effort to remember their name? Are they a dentist named Dr. Tusk?
- If the name can easily be associated with something visual – see the picture in your head, for example Cliff, House, Ford.
- Create a mental picture of this new acquaintance engaged with someone you know well, with the same name. "New Erin," is riding with your old cycling buddy Erin.

2. Praise others and make them feel important and valued in your presence and the presence of others. Be genuine, sincere and natural in your delivery of praise.

People generally like to hear two things, their name and praise for something they do or have done well. There is a very popular management principle that states, 'what gets rewarded, gets repeated'. Rewarding desired behaviors is more powerful than criticizing undesired behaviors. A positive approach motivates, while critical responses may only yield compliance, if you are lucky. In our workshops, we refer to praise and positive reinforcement as 'throwing confetti' on someone.

3. Be reliable. Reliability is what we do over time to meet our promises and keep our word. And, this is a fundamental element of building trust relationships.

Cement takes time to dry. It does not serve its actual purpose as a strong foundation until it does so. Trust takes time to strengthen too and your reliability is the warm air (which causes wet cement to dry) within our relationships. As you continue to keep your promises and deliver 'above their expectation', the other person's view of you strengthens and so does your personal charisma. Reliability is what permits relationships to survive rough spots and disappointments and is a cornerstone of the charismatic person.

4. Remember the things that the people in your personal network care about. Then showcase the value you place in their relationship by reflecting this knowledge when with them.

Today, there exist more tools than ever to help us manage client relationships. Whether leaders today are using social or non-social media, it's essential that you are familiar with the more popular available client relationship management tools, which is why we cover them extensively in our workshops. Let's discuss some of the easy ways to stay connected to our clients.

- The simple act of remembering a person's birthday is an acknowledgement of their importance to you. Send a hand written card, pick up the phone, drop-off a token gift, or join their Facebook comments, just to name a few.

- When they reach milestones such as a career anniversary or they achieved life-milestone goals that they were working toward such as running a marathon, congratulate them.
- Electronic card services such as BlueMountain.com or JacquieLawson.com allow you to set up a mailing list with reminder tools where you can automatically be reminded of these upcoming events. These tools also create a valuable personal touch.

While we may have good intentions, doing these things can become less important during our busy workday. But when we remember to act on these things, we create experiences for our customers that will help them remember us for years to come. Become a center of gravity by projecting personal charisma. Acquiring this skill and consistently engaging in the activities to support it, will serve you well.

Principle 4: Build your personal brand

Michael Goulian is an acrobatic pilot. Please look him up because he has built an exemplary online presence. Michael participates in air shows around the world and does the types of things with a plane that most seasoned pilots would find exhilarating. This pilot is in a class all his own and sometimes pulls 8 or 9 G's in some of his maneuvers. He also competes in Red Bull air races, perhaps the most dangerous type of flying that exists today. He lives the "How to Sell" 12 principles. For him, developing a strong personal brand is an intentional, everyday act. While he has attained rock star status in his field, his humility and kindness are your first impression when you meet him. At the end of one of his shows in South Florida, after crawling out of his small, hot aircraft, he stands for hours snapping photos with enthused onlookers, never having to be reminded to smile for the camera because that is all he does anyway. People who know or meet Michael can instantly describe how they feel about him, without hesitation. And, in every case, it will be a positive impression that spreads his brand. He is a successful businessperson because of his lasting reputation in his world and he reminds us of how we can also permit our brand to do some important heavy lifting for us.

We all experience the power of branding daily. Whether it's Coca Cola, Apple, Intel, BMW, Tide, a brand is a perception. It's the adjective that we associate with a company, product or service. Companies have spent large sums of marketing dollars to build and sustain a brand image. And as Malcolm Gladwell's "Tipping Point" formula suggests, we repeat, repeat and repeat again the message, we want to brand, to the stakeholders that can promulgate that message to the masses. Companies use television, celebrity endorsements, billboards, Internet message boards, memorable slogans and other forms of advertising to trumpet their brand, hoping that their intended message will stick. Yet, when we look at the actual construct of a brand, it is more about the customers' experience with the product or service over time, than anything else. It is also the accumulation of experiences that influence the perception of the brand. Therefore, each engagement we have with an agent of a company communicates the integrity of their brand.

Our personal brand works much the same way. People that we work with and know can describe us with a simple adjective or two. This is our brand to them and likely to others as well. When asked to describe us, they can usually do so in a few, confident words. The adjectives they use are the behaviors and characteristics that resonate the loudest to them over time. The best salespeople have created a reputation that precedes them. They are known for being punctual, competent, knowledgeable and helpful, an asset to their organization. They have accomplished this through consistently making, perhaps unknowingly, our twelve principles part of their performance DNA, especially the first principle. Here are some additional tips to help build your personal brand.

A. Take inventory of your behaviors with others.

Consider asking someone that you trust to share his or her honest assessment of your behaviors that both add to and subtract from your positive personal brand. Be prepared to accept what they say unprejudiced. Also be prepared to make changes that alter those negative behaviors they identify. If you are unsure about their judgment, test it by asking someone else you trust. This is all about personal improvement. Assessing your current behaviors and their impact on others is a vital element to this improvement process.

As trainers, we have spent more time in the area of peer-to-peer coaching as we have in any other skills development area. This is because of the accelerated breakthroughs that are derived from having a trusted observer give us constructive feedback on our actions. Make taking an inventory of your behaviors a personal brand fitness regimen.

B. Avoid negatives, criticism and sarcasm.

When we spoke of sales being the amplification of human nature and behavior, we need to acknowledge that we amplify both the good and the bad behaviors. Our good behaviors are discussed in our 12 Principles and before we go any further, we need to discuss some of those actions that may be well intentioned but yield negative results. First among them is complaining. While we may have many reasons to complain about things, does it really produce the result we desire? We can often witness the answer to this question at an airport gate when a plane is delayed or a restaurant where the quality of food or service do not meet expectations. We have watched someone melt down over unmet expectations. And we know how we feel when we are witnessing someone overreact with an outburst of anger or frustration. Do we believe the complainer is representing their personal brand in the best light as a result of their outburst? Complaining should only be reserved for those few instances where the outcome from it will be a positive transformation for you and others.

Criticism is another verbal crevasse. While we may criticize someone's behavior and call it "constructive" with the intent to help him or her, it's generally received negatively and often sets up a self-defensive reaction. Often, we do not even hear the response. The people we criticize take mental note and can engage in brew-and-stew thinking. That thinking manifests itself in downstream actions that could come days, weeks or months later when the critical moment is long in the past. We once coached a salesperson that criticized her own company in front of her customers so she could position herself as the hero. She did this to build herself up in the midst of her company's dysfunction. Unfortunately, her intention to position herself in a positive light eventually resulted in lasting damage to her company brand and the loss of her customer.

Sarcasm is a two edged sword. The intention is humor; the message is received as an insult. For example, a well-educated manager whose style was to use sarcasm to lighten the mood, during conference calls with his team in the field, he would often quip, "I know all of you are probably on your third martini by now." Unknown to him, one of his key field salesmen was a recovering alcoholic. While that salesman was able to put the sarcasm in its proper perspective, he still viewed the leader as insensitive and shallow. Not a good personal brand for any leader.

As we communicate with customers and co-workers, words are powerful. The weight of words and behaviors over time create perceptions, establishes intent and defines us in the eyes of others. We are not seeking human perfection, just consistent exhibition of the best human values.

As James Allen, a 19th century American Philosopher, author of *As A Man Thinketh*[9], once said, "The strong, calm person is always revered." It was true then and remains so today.

C. What is your online brand?

We have experienced being in front of a group of executives during a training session, and without warning, some of the participants confronted us with different aspects of our professional lives. None of which we mentioned during the class. It was immediately obvious that a quick Google search was the method and a laudable sense of curiosity was the motivation. These experiences motivated us to add a comprehensive personal online branding component to our "How to Sell Seminars". It is necessary that as sales professionals we control – best we can – our online personal brand. Our personal brand is the reputation we have through social media and how the web represents us. By taking control of our web presence, we can establish credibility beyond our direct network of associations. This is an essential part of personal branding for the 21st century professional.

As a start, we recommend using LinkedIn. Currently with approximately 364 million members worldwide, including executives from every Fortune 500 Company, LinkedIn is the world's largest professional network on the Internet. This is an effective resource, which will allow you to be seen by many in the light you prefer. More suggestions:

- Make sure you own "your name.com" and build your own website.
- Develop your own Wikipedia page
- Create your own YouTube channel or online video.

Remember, this is all about building your personal brand in such a way that you create a reputation that precedes you. People are using word of mouth, traditional and social media to learn about us. Let's do all we can to manage and maintain what the world says about us by managing our behaviors and social media messages.

Principle 5: Be Naturally Curious

"The important thing is not to stop questioning. Curiosity has its own reason for existing."

—Albert Einstein[10]

Curiosity is one of the most intriguing human traits. It was that trait that drove man across continents and into space. It advances science and technology, builds businesses and finds medical breakthroughs. Curiosity is a powerful force when we choose to unleash it for good purposes. So, we are naturally curious by nature, but how do we translate it into our success?

Brian Gazer, one of Hollywood's most successful producers, wrote a book called, "The Curious Mind: The Secret to a Bigger Life." He was responsible for such hits as, Tom Hanks — Splash, Russell Crowe — A Beautiful Mind, Tom Hanks — Apollo 13, and Denzel Washington — American Gangster and the television series "24" that turned actor Keifer Sutherland into the famed counter terrorist agent "Jack Bauer". Mr. Gazer wrote:

"More than intelligence, persistence or connections, curiosity has allowed me to live the life I wanted. Curiosity is what gives energy and insight to everything else I do. As soon as I realized the power of curiosity to make my work life better, I consciously worked on making curiosity part of my routine, I turned it into a discipline. And then into a habit."

In most sales training curriculum we are taught to develop a questioning strategy where we design a template from which to ask questions in an effort to understand the full landscape of a prospect's business needs. Depending upon the complexity of the sale, questions could facilitate a sale that is just transactional in nature and require only basic information to move forward. Someone wishing to purchase patio furniture may not require a deep conversation about needs and benefits. But a few questions about how they see themselves enjoying the furniture, in addition to, their view of the product specifications, such as size and color are essential. Now someone wishing to purchase a used corporate jet might require a more in-depth conversation. Questions about the aircraft specifications, use, budget, support structure and more would be in order. In both events, being naturally curious is an essential element to a successful outcome. In fact, the buyer accepts the display of genuine interest as an appealing quality.

Just as we can tell when someone is an exceptionally good listener, we can also tell when someone is being genuinely curious. We somehow can feel when someone is being authentic in their approach, that moment when they truly want to understand our challenges, issues, goals, and we are more inclined to give that person the information they seek. For the transactional sale, natural curiosity improves the chances of an initial-contact-to-close scenario. For a more complex sale, you certainly want a 'last look' when the purchaser has narrowed their choices.

Curiosity builds trust and converts a questioning session into a lively and productive conversation. It doesn't sound like an interrogation because it involves an exchange of information and interest. When we are questioning with genuine curiosity, we are more likely to explore all areas of interest with the customer and less likely to change the subject to an area of our own interest. Telling our own stories breaks the continuity of focused curiosity. Our conversations become more animated and interesting because we focus on subjects that interest our prospect or client.

Principle 6: Every Moment Counts, be in the moment

Do we live to work or work to live? We hear this question often. Our answer, just live and live well! What does this mean exactly? Be present, in the moment, aware of our surroundings and the people among us. React to what is happening near you. Respond to what people are saying or doing.

We often ask workshop participants, "What is the greatest skill a successful sales professional can possess?" The answer is resounding and predictable, "listening." You were not going to venture far into this book without seeing a treatise on the art of listening. Being an active, empathetic listener is perhaps the best compliment we give another person because we are telling them they are important and valued. It is obvious when we are exhibiting this skill at the highest level. Our eyes are fixed, our expression is supportive, our body language is open and our feet are planted in the direction of the speaker.

I (Charles) once worked with a salesperson that spent large parts of our conversations darting his eyes around the room in a random, nervous fashion. He was easily distracted and made me feel as though there was somewhere else he would rather be than speaking with me at that moment. Coaching this person to be in the moment wasn't easy. During a conversation about the art of listening, we were discussing frustrating situations in our lives. He told me that his wife would interrupt him during ball games on TV and be angry that he wasn't listening to what she had to say. I asked him to, just once for the entertainment of it, grab the remote and the next time she approached him this way he should turn off the TV and just focus on her. On a follow up coaching session he said, "I did as you said and turned off the TV when she came around the corner from the kitchen wanting my attention. He said, "...

the moment I turned off the TV, she stared at me with a momentary pause and said, what's wrong, did I say something wrong? No, I said, I just wanted to hear what you have to say. Please, sit down here and tell me what's on your mind." Well, we had one of the most intimate and open conversations that day and I can tell she really felt valued for being listened to" and with that, he realized the importance of focusing on others in the moment. Not only is it just good practice to be in the moment, every moment, for the enhancement of our personal brand, it will also help to build stronger relationships with people who value that trait. After all, aren't these the people with whom you wish to associate with anyway?

We realize this will be a work in process for a while as you work to be intentional with improving your listening skills. If we are truly paying attention to the world around us with open eyes and an open heart, we will experience the full breadth of life. Often the most rewarding of these moments are fostered by our interactions with others. Be in the moment and those around you will appreciate you for this quality.

Principle 7: Every person counts, let them know.

Have you ever met someone that made you feel as though you were the only other person in the room when you were speaking with them? How do you feel about them? This is the person we need to be. It is a compliment to the other person because it makes them feel important and becomes part of our personal brand. This Principle is supported by Principle 6 (Every moment counts).

Bob Littell, who is a noted author of the book, "The Heart and Art of Netweaving". He started a movement to create a business climate of Netweaving. His premise was simple and related to the pay-it-forward philosophy. In a typical networking environment, we are usually on the hunt for prospects. We endeavor to meet people that can help us achieve our objectives and help us to be more successful. When we introduce ourselves to a new person, our mindset is on the potential of this person becoming a client or a referral resource. Netweaving is the converse of that approach. When we meet someone, it is now our intent to find ways to help him or her be successful. As we are speaking to a Netweaving contact, we are considering introductions, referrals or testimonials we can offer that will help them. It requires us to be naturally curious and learn about that person and their business challenges. Once learned, we act on their behalf. These acts of true goodwill pay dividends because we are now creating champions in our lives — people motivated to help us win.

With this attitude, think of how first impressions of us would change. Becoming a Netweaver is a mindset change as well as forcing a definitive change of behavior. We are now making connections and introductions that we might have never made otherwise. We are strong promoters of both this philosophy and the attitude and action required to be this kind of altruistic person.

An executive with a Big 4 accounting firm exhibited this quality with true intent. He would say that he believed in the 3-foot rule. He defined it as, "…anyone within 3 feet of me will get a handshake, a greeting, an introduction, and a question about him or her." If a conversation broke out, it would be about them, not him. Having a mindset that says, 'It's not about me, it's about you' translates in our everyday conversations and ultimately our relationships. We are transparent as communicators, where people not only hear our words but understand our intent. People will know whether we are in it for them or ourselves.

A well-known vocal coach who had worked with many famous performers both in the movies and on Broadway, once said, it is easy to tell the difference between a professional and an amateur. He said that it was not whether they made money that defined the difference. There were many amateurs making a lot of money, just as there are many professionals not making a dime. The difference is evident by their focus.

Are they performing for them self or their audience? A true professional is performing for the audience's pleasure and the audience rewards the performer with their acknowledgement. It becomes easier to know when you are in the presence of a consummate professional by this definition.

The professional salesperson acknowledges others they come in contact with, listens to them, becomes involved in their expressions *in the moment* and makes them feel important and valued.

Principle 8: Manage your time

Time management is all about being organized and proactive which increases our ability to perform and become more successful. Time management will help to eliminate your mind of clutter and unproductive distractions. The modern guru of time management, David Allen in his book "Getting Things Done" covers the subject of managing your personal and professional time in wonderful detail. He shares the techniques necessary to be maximally efficient and relaxed whenever you need or want to be. We also have sage advice for the sales professional that will save time and speed up results based on our experience.

> *"Much of the stress that people feel doesn't come from having too much to do. It comes from not finishing what they've started."*
>
> —David Allen[11]

Do the difficult thing first. The difficult things we put off are usually the large pieces of unfinished business on our stack of things to do. And, as the quote suggests, it is the source of much of our stress. Stress wreaks havoc on our ability to perform. And we spend countless minutes and hours worrying about things.

Having coached professional salespeople for years. We have found that most worry about things that are left undone that could be accomplished right now. Stress kills memory, creativity and the ability to be in the moment with our clients. Put that most difficult task on the top of your list and just get it done. This will only increase your performance bandwidth — the mental capacity required to perform at your best.

Address the source of your stress directly. Stress is a time thief because of the time and energy we expend to fret over potential consequences and ramifications of high stress events or situations. If you are faced with a stressful event, find the root cause of your stress. Is there some action that you are putting off because it might be unpleasant? Be honest with yourself and handle the action that is causing your stress. Give yourself some tough love. If the stressful source is something in the future that you might dread, we have found that if you schedule a meeting with yourself, at some point in the near future, and title the meeting "Worry about this thing", it dissolves. Send an outlook meeting notice to yourself with the note, this is my hour to worry about this stressful event. Then just forget about it. You've already scheduled time to worry so you don't need to do that now or ever.

Build trust-based relationships to save time. If there is one time management 'sleeper' it is that we are more efficient with our time when dealing with people we trust. We just get things done faster when working with those with whom we already have strong relationships. Put building relationships on your to do list. Most of our to-do lists are all about accomplishing tasks. Handle this, finish that. Seldom are we intentional in creating work for ourselves by putting things on the list to improve relationships. Yet, we have established that the time spent in building trust relationships will yield big dividends over time and speed up results. So let's set out to be intentional in building and/or sustaining key relationships to keep them optimal.

This story is an example of how building relationships is the little known secret to effectively saving time. I (Charles) remember a tough supply chain manager that I once called on in a Fortune 200 account. We were often engaged in impactful price and service negotiations. I had received an anonymous tip that her husband was having a kidney transplant and the donor was their daughter. The day of the surgery, I had a to-do to call her and let her know that I was thinking about her and her family. No business was discussed on that call. That afternoon, she called me back and let me know that the patients were doing well. Her tone was excited as she spoke to me, "...the doctors said that when they set the kidney in with blood flow, it turned pink and there was an immediate positive response to the procedure." My intention for taking a moment to care was from a place of 'one human being to another'. I must also add that the negotiations that took place over the years with this tough business professional were transparent, smooth, fast and non-contentious. The outcomes truly balanced both the relationship and the results for both parties. Make building and sustaining relationships the most important thing you do and watch the pace of your ability to get things done quicken dramatically.

Clear your mail...daily. David Allen elaborated that there is a linear relationship between your stress level and the unresolved emails in your in-basket. Many of us boast about the number of active emails on our computer, this may be derived from some sort of strange psychology based on the notion that the higher the number of emails percolating in our active space, the higher our importance to the company. Make the goal of zero emails in your active box by the end of the day. Yes we feel the collective gasps from you as you read this. Yes, you may never achieve it, but try it. You will surprise yourself by finding ways to focus on the correspondence that truly requires your action. Delete, file, eliminate, delegate, accelerate and 'touch it once' are the mantras of the efficient mail handler. Make them your daily chant and watch your stress level melt to a manageable level.

Principle 9: Manage your relationships

If we only had one piece of advice to give to a young, aspiring sales professional to enable them to be most successful, we would tell them to build relationships based upon trust. As we said in the prior principle, manage your time; our inventory of strong relationships is our fast track to effectiveness. Here is where we slow down to speed up. Take the time to build relationships and then watch your ability to work with and through people you trust accelerate your achievements. Relationships are not static so they need constant nurturing and management.

Any 9th grade biology teacher can site the following law of nature; there are only two states in nature, you're either growing or decaying. There is no neutral state for all things living. The same law of nature can be applied to our relationships. They need to be touched and nurtured. Like soup on the warmer, that needs to be stirred every now and then to keep the bottom from burning, our business relationships need to be touched and nurtured to promote growth and avoid decay. To do this we should routinely call our account contacts and prospects.

For those of us that are working with longstanding relationships in active accounts where you are sustaining the business and mining for new opportunities, as they come up, develop a touch point plan that keeps you and your company known in the organization. Regularly contact people in the client company and constantly be the present resource. By doing this, your reputation grows beyond the perimeter of your known network in that organization.

After all, we want to be at the strategic planning table with our client when they are writing new specifications or developing their next new product. We can only do this by being top-of-mind, tip-of-tongue with our clients. This is accomplished by the never ceasing desire to expand the depth of our personal brand with those who are familiar with us while reaching out to others who are not familiar with us. Bob

Lucht, an aviation tire engineer was in every definition a professional salesperson. When engineers at Boeing, General Dynamics and other airframe manufacturing companies were planning a new design and needed reliable expertise and insight, Bob was their first call. He was their 'technology 911' and they knew that he would deliver value beyond their expectations during any discussion. Let me mention that he also was a charismatic communicator. Internal Account Managers would often receive calls from Bob saying, "the aircraft manufacturer is looking at a new derivative and I've shared some technology that could help them along. Now would be a good time to refresh your presence on the commercial business side of their organization." Bob built those relationships over the years and nurtured them. He would literally help them write the specification so that no one else but his company could deliver the solution.

Our relationships are our speed dial to success. If we could give just one piece of advice to any professional salesperson that would make them more successful, it would be to build strong business relationships, internal and external to your company, based on trust.

Principle 10: Take care of your customer

> *"It Costs Five Times More to Acquire a Customer than to Retain a Customer"*[12]
>
> *Praise for Loyalty Myths*
>
> —Keiningham, Vavra, Aksoy, and Wallard

Our customers expect us to take care of them. They are looking for us to keep our promise to deliver our products on time, provide world class service, and provide accurate documentation with quality support. They expect us to deliver on our promises. We only have one chance at first impressions and this cannot be squandered. So the campaign to sell ourselves extends beyond the start date of any contract. Every transaction with our customer needs to support and build our product and personal brand. Taking care of the customer needs to be our top-of-mind obsession.

Also, should you win the account and it represents a change of suppliers, it is not always easy path for our customers. There are costs, mostly hidden from us, associated with switching suppliers which are called "switching costs". These costs usually have to do with the additional work that comes with changing processes and relationships. We did not see the internal battles that were waged between the decision makers and stakeholders within our client's organization before we received our award letter. And we need to be sensitive to that dynamic after the change as well.

The business has been acquired and it is now time to turn the day to day operations to the support team. But during the campaign to win the business, we were selling our self, our company and the brands they represent. We made promises that said we were different and better than our competition and we will deliver world class service to support our world class products. So the customer now has an expectation about that forthcoming experience. Now is the time to exceed their expectations. The fact that we did not relax at this moment of commitment, but turned on the burners to set up exemplary service at the start will pay huge dividends. Here are some key practices to enable us to take care of, and keep, our customers.

Create a client experience that exceed their expectations

After the cake and confetti have been tidied up following the announcement of the win, it is time to begin creating the experience the client can anticipate going forward. This means orchestrating internal resources to assess and create processes that match the client's culture and structure. This is especially true where we are delivering products or services over time, where our solution is integrated in the solution they deliver to their customers.

Communications need to be prompt and complete. Relationships need to be positive and tight. Information needs to be accurate, relevant, and timely. And we need to create a 'partnership' feel with all we encounter. This is called being a world-class customer servant. In other words keep your promises, now.

We work with customer service professionals who perform supportive duties to customers after the sale is complete. They are just as responsible, perhaps even more so, for sustaining the quality brand for which your product or service is known. The good ones live by the 'get it done now' philosophy and are worth their weight in gold. This is the first tenet of delivering world-class customer service. As customers ourselves, we expect to have our calls, texts and mail returned right away. We expect positive, proactive responses, with a positive flair and so do our prospects and customers. Be the one who consistently delivers this kind of service to them.

Being reliable is a great personal brand to possess and a great time saver. For example, who is the most reliable company that you can think of? Is it FedEx, Amazon, Google? How do we reward them? Yes, that's right, we give them our repeat business. And that is how you will be rewarded also. And once reliability is established, you are rewarded with repeat business, unsolicited. That is how serving others saves time and promotes a positive personal brand.

Expand your network of client champions

Next, we need to know the individuals that we will be working with and their place within their organization. One sales professional demonstrated the value of this point by developing great relationships with the working level folks at her client account. She knew the buyer, finance accounts payable pro and the lead technical contact. The account was hitting on all cylinders, then the merger occurred. The management teams above her contacts were from the new parent company and they had strong relationships with her competitor. Her local contacts were unhappy with the changes and because of their relationship, they warned her of an upcoming re-bidding of the existing business. The coaching opportunity came in the form of a 'go big' strategy, where she would pull executives from her own company and deliver a capability presentation to the new management team. This was the time to establish credibility, present the positives of the past relationship and build some higher level relationships. Strong working level relationships are most important, but by continually building our network beyond our current contact comfort zone we will improve our chances to survive change through a larger relationship base.

Go the extra mile

In creating a valued client experience, clients know and remember when you are delivering over and above their expectation. Your customer will know and remember when they observe you performing this way. This means you must become an advocate for your customers. While you do represent the best interests of your own company, you are also the voice of the customer in your own company. Do not apologize for playing that role. Just remind your stakeholders that you will be representing their voice as part of any decision making or problem solving process. By helping your company see situations and actions from the customer point of view, you will be adding value to any internal action that affect the customer.

Know your customer

In order to take care of your customer, we should first know as much about them as we can. So, what is it that we really need to know to advance our opportunities? The obvious things are a great place to start.

We need to know more about the client company, its people, its products, the reason for its existence, its history, its future and its relationship to us. Through our workshops on account planning, we have come to realize that there is a balance between the amount of research and data collection that is necessary to truly know the customer and the time we need to perform our salesperson duties. It's a big charge and takes a campaign mentality.

Let's start with the customer's vision, mission and values. I remember one company where we were seeking additional business whose main value was to deliver packages on time. They expected the same from their vendors. Yet we were the first vendor to actually mirror their value and propose severe penalties for late deliveries in our proposal, thus guaranteeing our performance. We were not the lowest price but because we mirrored what they valued most, we were the best choice.

A company's mission statement represents what the company does. The vision statement represents how they intend to perform their missions. Their values guide their behaviors. Most buyers you will meet will not have committed their company mission statement to heart. Knowing their mission statement is not intended to impress anyone, but rather to acknowledge the focus of the executive management.

Take inventory of the company's culture. Are they process driven or do they leap from one transaction to another? Do their vendor facing people value relationships or do they operate at arms' length and value accurate and timely information. This is important as we engage with them from prospect to client is all about matching expectations and delivering to what the client organization values.

We should also know our customer's customers if we are working in a B2B space. The customers they serve are called their value chain. As professional salespeople, it is important to know how their customers use the products or services that are imbedded in our client's value chain. Knowing your prospects' value chain gives you an advantage in any negotiation and is certainly a differentiator from your competition.

We worked with a client that had great difficulty managing the change to a global invoice payment process after the start of the new agreement. The account went into a significant past due situation and management on both sides became irritable. This was not a good place to be on for a startup. The account executive became personally involved in the process to make corrections, solve problems, and keep the teams amicably talking. He then set up a future date certain for a success dinner that rewarded both teams once the past dues were cleaned up. The teams worked toward the dinner date and achieved the goal. In this way, the account executive went the extra mile, became an advocate, expanded his network and celebrated the success. Remember, customers buy more than products, they buy experiences.

Principle 11: Know your products

Gaining product knowledge is a work in progress, always. Most companies that invest time in sales professionals are constantly providing 'hard skills' training that bolsters product knowledge. Our professional credibility comes from the depth of our ability to link product features and functionality to a prospect's need. When presenting solutions to our clients we need to be able to link the facts and features to relatable benefits and payoffs. This requires us to have a deep knowledge of our products so that we can communicate those links in the moment without hesitation. The need to be accurate and reliable is also crucial to sustaining our credibility. We cannot misrepresent what our products and services can do.

While working with the sales team of a major charge card company, I (Andre) realized they had only minutes to conduct a sales conversation with a prospect, and the value of product knowledge was never more evident. They would make an initial contact with a prospect, ignite a conversation about the prospect's business issues and delve into their financial structure to identify needs, payoffs and benefits. When successful, the average length of contact was approximately 7 to 12 minutes. The features of the card were exhaustive and memorizing them would be a challenge for anyone in the field. Yet, these professionals were able to match a specific business need to a card feature and describe an outcome with brevity, clarity and persuasion. Add to that, the salesperson had to ensure that their words were in compliance with the strict regulations of an offering in this type of financial transaction, so they needed to be accurate and flawlessly truthful.

Where do we begin with our product knowledge? We would start with the most popular products and work to understand their physical characteristics, their specifications, how customers use them, their strengths and weaknesses and the messaging that the company uses to promote the product brand. From this we create 'reserve power' for our conversations with clients and a confidence to delve to a level of depth that promotes clarity and interest. For more complex solutions, we can always insert subject matter experts in the conversation to take the technical discussion to a new level.

While we are huge advocates of having strong product knowledge, many salespeople plateau because they rely too heavily on a presentation of features, facts and functionality of their products. This leads to feature dumping and is a trap that will likely result in an objection or even a rejection of our attempts to generate interest from our prospects. Product knowledge is key to advancing the sale as long as that knowledge is shared in a targeted way to support the presentation of our solution to a well-defined prospect need.

As we will discuss in detail later in the Sales Process chapter, our prospects and customers want to be convinced with compelling evidence that support the perceived benefits of our products. This requires not only an understanding of how the product is used but also the confidence to comfortably engage in this conversation in a manner that will make us more interesting, convincing and entertaining when presenting our solutions. This is a valuable differentiator from the competition.

We should develop our own method for organizing product information in a handy reference. Constantly study how customers use our products/services and how it benefits them. Interview happy customers and find out why they love our products to give us words to use in our prospecting contacts and to help us sell ourselves on the value of our solutions.

Principle 12: Know Your Competition

Yes, the competition is also conducting strategic planning meetings to grow their business and take market share — your share. Picture their war room, with a big board with your loyal accounts listed as a target account for them to go after. Their best prospect is your current customer. They are scheming to build relationships, generate interest and leverage their strengths against your weaknesses in order to take some or all of your business away from you. So, we cannot ignore the competition in our planning processes. Know their strengths and weaknesses. Predict their thoughts about what opportunities they might be seeking. The marketplace is giving us clues as to their behaviors and intentions, so pay attention.

During tenure in sales and as a sales manager, I (Charles) always kept a current organization chart of my competitors' organization and I always expected the reps that reported to me to have the same. As well, I needed to be able to understand my competitors' strategic drivers and their go-to-market messaging. Why did I feel this was important? As part of qualifying my prospects, I found it essential to determine how the competition might approach them or where their weaknesses were in their solutions being offered to my prospect. While my messaging focus was toward the client's needs, I also endeavored to subtly and honestly illuminate my competitor's weakness, to cast doubt and alter their brand where it made sense. Being able to identify consequences of choosing or staying with a competitor often creates the sense of urgency to encourage your prospect to 'buy now', from you.

We should know what product performance comparisons exist between our competitor's products and ours. Ask our prospects who have used our competitor's products for information about how they outperform and underperform ours. We must be able to compare our services in the same manner. If there is data that gives us head-to-head comparisons of our product performance versus theirs, file it and use it. Many companies have their product/services support group capture performance data for the major competitors from their customers and keep the data in a library accessible by salespeople and support staff.

There are two distinct schools of thought regarding how to approach discussions about our competition – one school, and the most popular teaching, is to avoid at all cost, make no negative comments about our competition. The other school supports using the weaknesses of our competition against them when possible. We choose neither school of thought. We believe it is productive to take the middle ground.

Let's use unobtrusive messaging to illuminate our strengths over a competitor's weakness. If a competitor has a branding problem due to a negative perception in the market place, consider bolstering that negative image. For example, while working with an industrial coating company with a strong focus on the customer as the cornerstone of their customer engagement process, we learned they have a competitor who was perceived by the industry as "arrogant". Apparently, their approach was one that felt like, "You should feel privileged to have us as your vendor," according to some customers. Why not share the stories from customers, taking the opportunity to highlight our focus in contrast. If they have had similar experiences it will strike a cord and if not, they will be sensitive to it. Simply be tactful and subtle!

A sales rep shared the following story that speaks to the need to pay attention to details. He was calling on a target account that was loyal to a competitor. He had a decent relationship with both the purchasing agent and the operations person who was responsible for the use of his product type. He noticed that the competition would provide a dish full of bagels and cream cheese on the last Friday of every month to the purchasing group. They really seemed to value the gesture and it was great exposure for the competitive brand. The astute rep did state to the buyer that if the competition ever ceased to provide the monthly bagel treat to please let him know and he would be glad to step in and take over. Well, within a few months the competitor decided to stop the practice. The enterprising sales rep was able to replace the popular treat and ensured that each delivery from the local bagel company was accompanied with a placard with his company's name prominently displayed on the tray along with the food. When the next request for proposal was issued, there was no contest and the salesman had the inside track and his deal. Paying attention to details could pay dividends from the most unlikely places.

We should study our competitors as time allows. Select a Google alert for them by name just to stay current on their newsworthy events. (https://www.Google.com/alerts). Try to discover where they have strong alliances and good experiences and where they don't. Keep an active competitor file open and current. Obtain their price lists and product/service collateral for our file. These activities will pay credibility dividends with those clients who are seeking advice from an industry 'expert or maven.'

CHAPTER 3

The Sales Process

Why do we need a process? We believe that salespeople like a process and have a desire to know the step they are in during the evolution of the sale. Following our sales process will keep you organized, will help you think before you speak, and drive you towards the commitment phase with structured confidence.

W. Edwards Deming, the father of modern quality, once explained why products fail[13]. It is caused by variation in the product's manufacturing, materials, use or maintenance processes. A whole quality movement was built around that very thought and still survives today. This movement demands great effort to reduce or eliminate variation in each step of manufacturing. For every successful product or service, there is a refined, uniform process followed and executed with consistent precision. This also could be true for salespeople who want to match their valued solutions to business needs.

We have constructed a sales process to help you understand the simple steps to advance your sales conversations and opportunities. The process flows from one step to the next and each element builds on the next. These steps show the natural progression used to build most business relationships. They are:

1. **Build a Bond – connect, build trust, promote cooperation.**
2. **Explore the Gap – Be curious, be a consultant, explore needs.**
3. **Build a Bridge – Reveal buying motive.**
4. **Bridge the Gap – summarize needs, present your solution.**
5. **Walk the Bridge – handle objections, motivate the sale.**
6. **Close the Gap – get their commitment.**

In this chapter we will expand on each element of the sales process.

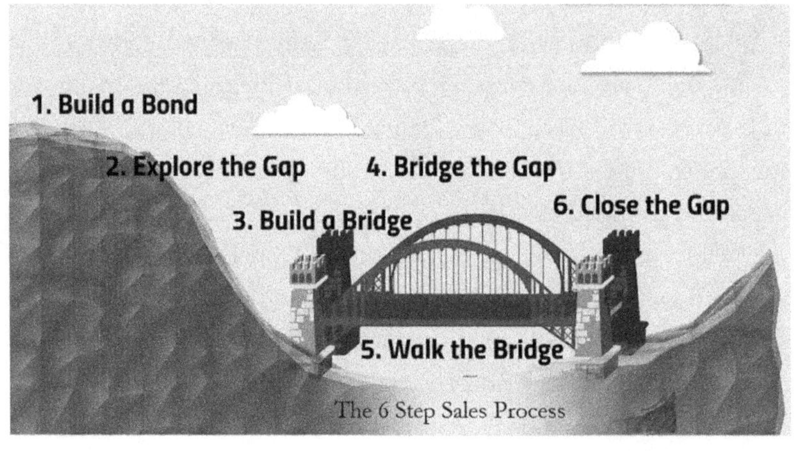

The 6 Step Sales Process

STEP 1: BUILD A BOND

This step is essential to any sales process. We do not sell in a vacuum. We need information to effectively sell and thus we need the prospect's cooperation to obtain the details we will use to construct a solution. We must consult before we construct our solution. And we must connect before we consult.

We know that first impressions happen quickly, often before we open our mouth, and we are transparent as communicators. So what we believe and think, we are communicating to others. We need to do some internal work to start the process of building trust with those we are meeting. The internal work is moving beyond 'what's in it for me' and onto 'what's in it for them'. With this clear intention, we are now prepared for any contact with anybody. Remember, curiosity is the essential element that will keep our attention on them.

A salesperson from a Software data company that provides patient management software programs for hospitals went to visit a long-standing client. They had a long business relationship although the business there was declining and they had missed some opportunities to add new products in new departments at this hospital chain. The purpose of the visit was to introduce himself as the new rep for the account and it was obvious that the buyer was lukewarm to this introduction. During the early part of introductions, the new rep asked the buyer about her experience with her software company. The buyer, without hesitation, said, "I just didn't like the last representative you had." When asked why, the buyer only elaborated with this statement, "I did not like his negative energy." Let's face it; it doesn't get any more basic than that. The customer has to, at the very least, like the representative.

First impressions become lasting impressions. Good ones are easy to sustain, bad ones are hard to change. From the moment they cast eyes on us our clients are assessing us. They are taking all of us in before we even open our mouth. Here are some simple tactics to focus on, in the early stages of a relationship that will improve our chances.

TIPS FOR CREATING A POSITIVE FIRST IMPRESSION

- Project a positive image — smile more, be friendly
- Keep your eyes up and calm
- Start with enthusiasm — an enthusiastic greeting pays dividends
- Stand Straight, Start Strong
- Focus on the customer — It's all about them, not us

Having a conversation is the most basic of human activities. And having an enjoyable one with another person that exhibits mutual interest and energy has its own pleasing rhythm. We all should do this as a matter of routine. The sales conversation has a different edge and requires the salesperson to become interested in someone else's world with the intention to understand and provided advice. Yet, so often we do not have the patience or time to engage in a conversation with genuine interest in what the other person has to say. We have observed that the art of listening to and being genuinely interested in other people's point of view has become the exception and not the rule.

As humans, this is not unusual. We compare the value of our engagements with the time necessary to have them and assess whether to continue or discontinue the engagement. Our prospects also do this when we engage them. They ask themselves, "Should I continue to talk with this person? Where is this conversation going? What else could I or should I be doing right now?" It is our responsibility as sales professionals to make every interaction with a prospect count – for them! We must engage the prospect in a manner that delivers value from the beginning. The prospect must feel that our interaction is valuable to them from the onset or they will look for the first opportunity to get back to their previously established priority list.

Therefore, the first step in our sales process, building a bond, involves engaging our prospect or customer at the point of maximum value to them. How do we accomplish this seemingly elusive feat? Let's start with **Principle 6: "Every Moment Counts, be in the moment"**. This sounds simple, and it is, but it does take effort.

For example, when I (Andre) started my sales career, I began as a stockbroker trainee, at a small Wall Street investment firm. Like every other stock broker in that day, I made 200 + cold calls per day and they all sounded like very much like this – "Mr./Mrs. prospect, this is Andre O'Brien, calling from Wall Street and I can make you money". Every stockbroker in the United States was calling on the same "high net worth group of potential investors hoping to have the opportunity to begin a relationship. One day, I decided to do something different, and the difference resulted in a learned lesson, I have carried with me since that day.

One day, I made the decision that a small company headquartered in New Jersey was the investment idea I would introduce to my potential new clients. It had a proprietary new technology in the area of Magnetic Resonance Imaging – MRI's. I was excited about it, but that was not enough. Could you imagine me calling high net worth potential clients, for example, executives at Sara Lee, and discussing the wonderful investment opportunity in MRI technology? I would sound like every other broker calling them with the next great idea, trying to explain the brilliance of the technology and doing my best to convince them that I knew better than all of my competition. I was determined to be unique so I asked myself a series of questions.

- Who would sincerely care about this company and its technology?

- Why would they care?
- Out of this list of prospects, who has significant disposable income to invest?

I decided that radiologists, would be the group to call. They were the medical specialists who would most be impacted by this advancement and they earn approximately $500,000/year. My cold calls now sounded like this:

"Dr. Prospect, I am Andre, calling from Wall Street. I have had the pleasure of speaking with many of your colleagues, specialists in the field of radiology, regarding an advancement in MRI technology that essentially speeds up the shutter speed of an MRI, virtually giving you a moving image. I would like to send you some information for your review and call you back to discuss the investment opportunity this advancement presents us. Would this be okay with you?" Why did virtually, every doctor I engaged say yes? Because I strategically positioned the value of the information. This is what I knew about the group of people I started to prospect: Radiologists earned approximately $500, 000 a year, they were required by their personal and professional integrity to stay abreast of all new advancements in their field and they took enormous risk daily as part of their jobs. I also knew that the possibility of a more advanced MRI machine would help them make better diagnoses.

Respectfully, these specialists were also driven by their own egos to confirm or debunk my claim of the existence of a new technology in their industry, of which they were unfamiliar. In short, they owed it to themselves to at least review my information. The truly amazing part of this experience for me was the opportunity to speak with these doctors during my follow-up phone call and hear their excitement when they learned this technology was not only real but also represented a ground floor investment opportunity.

When I made my follow-up phone call, and the doctor acknowledged that they not only read the information but were intrigued by it, I simply stated, "Dr., since you are the expert in this area of science, I will continue to forward information to you and ask that you to assess its continued viability. As long as we both believe that this technology is promising, we can build our investment position in the stock and continue to grow that position until the rest of Wall Street discovers this opportunity and buys these shares from us at a much higher prices. I recommend starting our investment position with a $10,000 investment, will this work for you or would you like to start with more?"

The number of daily cold calls were reduced with significantly better results because I knew my customer the way you must know yours. For the record, once I had the formula for success, I simply repeated it. For example, I found investment ideas that were of interest to Anesthesiologist and Immunologist and simply executed a rinse and repeat. During this process, I had the privilege of developing relationships with some of the finest people in our medical profession. Also, when the financial markets were underperforming, these clients felt comfortable continuing to take my advice as a Trusted Advisor because of the consultative nature of our relationship – we were in it together.

We should always engage our prospects where they are, demonstrating value with every step. Let's discuss how we get to know our customer. We must make every effort to walk in the shoes of our prospect so we may gain a perspective on what is most important to them in their daily professional role.

The Goal of Building a Bond: The Trust Relationship

Trust is the foundation of every successful relationship. It is built from the first moment of engagement and constructed over time with consistent and reliable forethought and action.

When we have trust, it becomes an accelerator to getting things done in our life. When we establish trust with someone, our ability to get things done with and through that person just kicked into high gear. Have you ever asked someone to help you move at some point in your life? No doubt, you asked someone you trusted, usually a family member or friend. Let us guess, there was pizza involved at some point? So how did the conversation go? Because you were asking someone you trust, the conversation was probably short and precise, as was the response. When considering those you trust in your business network and the way that you are able to communicate and work with them, it becomes clear that trust relationships yield an unmistakable advantage. In Steven Covey's, Speed of Trust, he states "*Financial success comes from success in the market place, and success in the marketplace comes from success in the work place. The heart and soul of all of this is trust...trust is the ultimate root and source of our influence.*

Since we are spending some time on the subject of trust, it is a good time to offer what one expert on the subject has to say. David Maister, Harvard Professor, created the "Trust Equation"[14] in an attempt to identify the elements of trust and to place metrics for each element to gauge their contribution to the end result.

The model is simply this:

David Maister's Trust Equation

$$\textbf{TRUST} = \frac{\textbf{Credibility + Reliability + Intimacy}}{\textbf{Self-Orientation}}$$

The elements simply stated are:

- Credibility—is what we say and how we say it. It requires us to be knowledgeable, accurate, honest and relevant.

- Reliability—is what we do over time. It requires us to be consistent, on time, a promise-keeper, proactive and unselfish.
- Intimacy—is the level of safety people feel while talking to us about their business issues. We should strive to be insightful, driven by our ability to be interested, interesting, motivated, genuinely curious, and an effective communicator. Empathy is an effective synonym and can be stated as "you care about the client, and they know it." They must know that you care about them for this to register dividends
- Self-Orientation—is our proclivity to focus on ourselves and not others. This should be minimized as much as possible.

Mr. Maister stated that the equation should be used with a numerical value for each element that result in a high number representing the value of Trust. This means the values for credibility, reliability and intimacy need to be high, while self-orientation (focus on our own goals) needs to be low as it is the denominator. Our team has presented the Maister model for years in various sales workshops because we believe that trust is the foundation of every successful relationship and should be the intent of every professional salesperson.

Knowing the elements of trust is powerful and frames the way we approach our clients and prospects. Trust can be considered a new language. Since we have established that trust is the first goal of any burgeoning relationship, let's position our conversation to promote trust. First and foremost, we need to establish how we earned the right to be in room with the client.

The first element of the model is credibility or what we say and how we say it. In building trust early on, we must establish credibility for ourselves and explain in a concise way how that has earned us the right to offer a solution to our client's need(s). This initial statement has been termed a "position" or "credibility" or "capability" statement. Better known as an "elevator pitch". In the next section, we will discuss some ways that you can construct these statements with an exercise to cement your ability to deliver them in the moment of need. Most importantly, remember to add the passion and enthusiasm in your statement to establish credibility. Your client will be gauging 'how you say it' more than the words you use.

Establishing your credentials

Every buyer needs to know how you and your company have earned the right to make a solutions presentation before they give you the keys to their kingdom. This requires you to establish credibility in the form of a credibility statement – or the 'elevator pitch'. We find most have not disciplined themselves enough to sit down and actually script one out. Rather, they rely on their ability to communicate off the cuff to do the work for them. Prepare for success. Use a solid structure when introducing your professional capabilities. We have a simplified structure to make it easy to develop such a statement in the moment. When asked, tell me about yourself, just answer these questions:

a. Who am I (we)?
b. What do I (we) do?
c. What can I (we) do for you?
d. Who else have I (we) helped?

Example for a personal introduction…

a. I am Jeff Collins and
b. I am committed to helping you and your team achieve a higher level of professional sales development.
c. I have helped successful people, like yourself, become even more successful by refining their sales skills so they can comfortably

use an end-to-end sales process that will increase both their conversion rates and personal income.

d. I have worked with thousands of individuals like you and have watched them sell more and produce more income at an accelerated pace and I believe you may be able to realize similar results.

Example for an introduction of your company....

a. We are Acme Widgets
b. We work with companies such as yours to help you increase inventory turns and maximize your return on investment and working capital.
c. Since you have a need for a higher margin and a faster moving widget for your retail customers, we are uniquely qualified to supply this need.
d. One company, like yours, that we recently worked with realized a 26% increase in sales and decreased their inventory costs by 19% in just 18 months with our just-in-time, turn-key service. We would like to help you have more working capital through lower inventory costs, just as they did.
e. **Special note: Once we share examples of the specific results others have achieved, we must be mindful not to make promises that could cause our prospects to question our credibility. If we do not know enough about our prospect's situation to promise them specific results then we should say the following: "We are not sure if you will achieve these same results, but that is why we appreciate the opportunity to learn more about your situation. This will help us to see what is possible for you." Then proceed to Sales Process Step 2 – Explore the Gap.

Statements such as these are essential for establishing credibility, earning the ability to ask probing questions and demonstrate experience with the client's key challenges. They become a springboard to asking more probing questions.

TIPS FOR BUILDING TRUST

- Introduce yourself with credibility
- Speak the truth
- Find common ground
- Demonstrate an empathetic demeanor

Summary for Building a Bond

Once we have established our credibility by what we say and how we say it, we can then build on that foundation to perform consistently and reliably. Let's be sure to demonstrate we care about the customer by word and deed. Customers should get a sense from the very beginning of the relationship about our intentions of meeting their needs.

STEP 2: EXPLORE THE GAP

Another name for the gap that we must explore is "client's need". It is the action the client must take to move from their current business situation to their desired business situation. There is some deficiency in their current situation that has created the need for our product or service. Or, perhaps there is an improvement in cost, quality or efficiency that represents an incremental advantage the client can leverage with your product or service. Your task is to explore what that deficiency or advantage is and sell to it.

For consumer products such as computers or mobile phones, the need could be as simple as a technology enhancement that represents improved quality or functionality such as memory or operating speed.

For the more complex sale such as system software or capital equipment, the advantages or deficiencies may be more complex. Consumers often make their decisions to buy an upgraded product around the dining room table, whereas large organizations identify gaps and make decisions to change suppliers at the boardroom level. For large organizations, the decision is usually an outgrowth of a goal to save money or improve quality. Someone at the department level is told to find the savings or quality improvement and that is why Request for Proposals (RFP's) are released. At some point, most of the advantages for the client reside in the categories of cost, quality or time, and our exploration will often begin and end here. We must become comfortable exploring needs at all levels of an organization to consider ourselves accomplished.

Therefore, we need to conduct conversations that balance skillful questioning and insightful commenting to determine the basis for their decision to change. These conversations take place every day, all around us, and the ones that are planned, organized, focused and process driven will deliver the best result. Our experience tells us that many salespeople do not go into these conversations with a plan. Often they are simply looking for a few key pieces of information – a search driven by a handful of superficial questions that will deliver questionable results. Having a broad plan, which includes a well-prepared questioning strategy and delving into these conversations is paramount to our success. Let's examine a way to ask questions that will yield the key information in a thorough and efficient way.

The Art of Questioning

> *"Successful people ask better questions, and as a result, they get better answers."*
>
> —Anthony Robbins[15]

Imagine that we are a business owner and we are interviewing a prospective consultant to come in and reconstruct part or all of our business. That potential consultant is sitting across the table from us and we are assessing their potential to be a "thinking partner" in our business. Before we give them the keys to our business kingdom, there are a few things we expect from this prospective consultant. We will want them to demonstrate credibility and help us feel confident that they are qualified to give us advice. This would come in the form of their credentials that gives factual information about their service and evidence on how they have helped other companies. Their ability to communicate this message clearly and confidently will also reinforce their credibility.

Once they have established how they have earned the right to be at the table, we would expect them to question us and stay in this mode for some time and really dig in to understand our business. We will not allow this individual to change our business until we know they have the ability to help us as evidenced by their proven track record and their understanding of our business landscape, challenges and needs. Should they offer a solution too soon, they will have shot themselves in the foot and lost credibility. And we would respond with a resounding, "Next candidate please!"

We must approach our questioning with our prospects and clients in this way. Call it being consultative and by all means be naturally curious. We need it, our customers want it, and it speeds up the whole process of selling.

I (Charles) remember when my son was 17 and was going to his first prom. He and I have always had a great relationship and he actually did take my advice from time to time. This was one of those times. He asked me what he should talk about with his date at dinner. He was not a wallflower by any means, but did have the same self-doubts that any 17 year old might have and lacked the confidence that comes with youthful courtship skills. I simply said, "Just ask her about things she is interested in. When you find her particularly energized about a subject, just stay there with her and explore that subject. If she wants to talk about her twin sister and you don't care about that, don't act bored, just match her positive emotional energy and find out more." Well he came home and said the advice was the key to a great evening. "I don't think she knows much about me, but she said I was one of the easiest people to talk to she has ever known. She really likes me!" Isn't that so true for us as well? The best conversationalists are the ones who spend more time listening to someone than those who just speak or brag on about themselves.

There is a method to asking the right questions, at the right time, and in the right way. It's just a matter of knowing how to begin and where to move from there. The purpose of asking questions goes beyond just our curiosity to understand more about their business. At some point, we will need to be able to match the benefits of our product to something they need. Let's face it, we already know what they need, how they can get it, how soon, how much and by what means. We are way ahead of them. So our questioning is a way to let them catch up with us. We are in essence 'slowing down to speed up.' This also gives us the opportunity to confirm any assumptions we have made and discover all opportunities presented by this gap.

What are the best questions to ask?

Most any standard sales training curriculum covers the types of questions that are available to us. Closed ended, open ended and thought provoking ("Impact") questions which represent the palate of question types that are available to us to enhance our exploration and uncover information to build our case.

TIPS FOR ASKING QUESTIONS...

- Use open-ended questions to discover.
- Use close-ended questions to validate information, confirm or shift gears.
- Use impact questions to identify benefits.

Closed ended questions are those that elicit a one, two or three word response. How long have you been in business? Are we on the right track? These questions are valuable when we are trying to validate some specific information. Or, they work well when we need to shift gears or get assurance that we are moving in the right direction. We like to think of them as questions that get the prospect to practice saying yes. Far too often, they are the most frequent type of question that salespeople ask. This results in a stilted conversation flow and makes obtaining important information much more difficult. If we find ourselves here, we will be doing most of the "heavy lifting". Let's make it easier on ourselves and avoid that trap.

Our seminar exercises permit you to discover your propensity to ask open vs. closed ended questions. We use open, closed and impact questions in tandem to obtain information that permits us, at some point, to summarize their needs.

What am I trying to learn from my client?

We question our clients to determine their needs. For many reasons, they usually don't just voluntarily offer their needs to us in a nice package, so we must do the work necessary to help them. A prospect's needs are usually imbedded in their day-to-day operations. So a broad understanding about their operations is a must. Our questioning should be designed to understand their business challenges and issues as a good starting point. Are they trying to increase profits, sales, inventory turns, client loyalty, new customers, associate productivity or working capital? Are they trying to decrease waste, unused manufacturing capacity, slow moving inventory, and product non-conformance or employee turnover? The answers to these questions are where their needs reside. We should also explore their areas of operational responsibility in addition to their strategic plans and initiatives for glimpses into their needs. During this discussion we want to gain an understanding of the following:

- What is their current business situation?
- What is their desired future business state?
- What would be the impact on them and their business when their future state is achieved?
- Why have they not yet achieved their future state?

What are Impact questions, and how do I use them?

Asking great questions is both a skill and an art form. Some of us have developed an innate sense for asking just the right questions at the right time while others must work a little harder at it. The next type of question, called an *impact* question, usually needs a little practice no matter the skill level. These questions can drive the conversation to a new level of insight and secure information necessary to increase the odds of success.

Impact questions are open-ended, deliberate and thought-provoking. They challenge the client to make comparisons, project an outcome, visualize possibilities and communicate feelings. Impact questions require the prospect to think deep and often cement credibility by causing the prospect to consider situations and outcomes not explored by our competition.

Before diving into a questioning structure, create a plan of engagement before reaching out to the client. Developing a few impact questions and having a good sense of the direction you want to pursue is a good practice. Just as we teach in our negotiations workshop, the one who is most likely to win is the one who is most prepared.

Let's examine a way to structure our questions to get the best result. Here's what we want to do. First, understand the landscape of their world. How does it work and what are their strategic initiatives. What is driving their business? Do they want to grow, consolidate, launch into new markets, or take more market share from a competitor? While these things might not obviously be directly related to what our products or services bring to them, they are very important drivers for their business. And, if we are astute, we will find the links and discuss them with the client later.

There is a difference between what we sell and what our customers buy. This is a bold statement that requires some explanation. We may sell copiers but our customer buys reliable, efficient printing solutions. We may sell medical software, but our customer buys accuracy and transparency. You see where we are going? When we are seeking to understand needs in our questioning phase, we cannot just stop at the obvious need at the surface; we must understand the value chain and how our product impacts our customers' customer. This is often where the real benefit of our solution reside.

I (Charles) met with a senior executive at a social event for a major airline whose name would be familiar to all of you. We were having a great discussion about some of the challenges facing the airline industry at that time. He told me that one of the drivers for their business was an airline term called 'dispatch reliability'. You know, that is the term that is used to describe when planes land on time or are late. The impact of plane's being late was huge for airlines. Because when a plane is late leaving and arriving, there are stiff penalties. As well, the flight crews have to be at their next station on time or they have to make adjustments. Just think of the last time you were at the gate when your plane was late. Happy place, right? The ripple effects are very costly to an airline and can cost as much as $25K an hour. Multiplied over a year, this costs large airlines tens of millions of dollars. And, "by the way," he said, "replacing a tire is the number one 'mechanical' reason for taking a delay for us right now." I asked him how much the tire events cost his airline and when he told me, it was more cost that the whole tire program was worth. "Why do you remove so many tires at the gate?" I asked. "Well, when they are worn, mechanics and the pilots have the power to make a decision to remove them." Over the course of the next few months we sat down and devised a joint program where removals could happen at an 'overnight maintenance base'. We worked on longer life treads and worn tire limits that gave them latitude for removals at a more convenient time, without causing delays. Because of that work, our business grew with them over the years as we found ourselves holding court at their strategic planning table. Not a bad position to be for a tire supplier at a major airline.

Our questions should at some point turn to what is at stake for their company and for them personally should they succeed in improving a process, saving money or solving the need that would ultimately be a result of using our product or service.

How much time should I spend asking questions?

In some instances, you have only minutes to acquire the information, summarize the need, present the solution and close the deal. For many of us, the sales cycle takes days, months or years. The key is to find the sweet spot that is right for your business. As a professional, you are already good at sensing the energy of the conversation and the level of engagement of the client. So use your guts here.

If you are expecting us to place an absolute limit on the amount of time to ask questions, you will be disappointed. It's not about the time, it's about getting the "need" right. If you are truly exploring with an interest to help solve an open issue, they will give you the time necessary. And, depending on the health of the relationship, they will help you with this expedition to reach the point where you can summarize their needs.

Many less seasoned salespeople are tentative when engaging their prospects and believe that they will give them very little time for questioning. Their suspicion becomes reality as they rush through their questions without a patient eye toward the goal. Buyers are astute and can read our intent and sincerity.

The consequence of not staying in the questioning mode long enough might lead you to miss the 'true' need or some of the anticipated objections. The best time to handle an objection is before it comes up. So our questioning should include probing for those potential objections that we suspect might arise. If they have had a bad experience with our product or service in the past, it is best to deal with it during the questioning part of the conversation, rather than at the close.

How do I keep their interest while probing for the information I need?

The answer to this question is not rocket science. Our level of interest is on display when we ask our client questions about themselves, their business and goals. As we are uncovering business challenges and issues, we are also discovering areas of concern to the client. Tune in to their energy and feed it. This is our opportunity to understand where we can make an impact for our client. If the conversation energy starts to wane, then change course. In John Maxwell's, "*Developing the Leader Within You*"[16] course, John Maxwell offers an easy-to-remember guide to better listening skills. He refers to it as the "Ladder to Better Listening," with "LADDER" being an acronym for the skills we need in order to listen to and understand others.

TIPS FOR BEING AN EFFECTIVE LISTENER – USE THE LADDER

- L—Look
- A—Ask Questions
- D—Don't interrupt
- D—Don't change the subject
- E—Manage our emotions
- R—Responsive listening

Maintain eye contact with the customer during the discussion. This is a very simple instruction, and a difficult task to execute. A brief glance away during the discussion can send all the wrong messages. Asking questions gives us the best chance to understand our customer's situation, and helps them to feel that we care. So do not interrupt your customer. Maxwell says, "It's just as rude to step on people's ideas as it is to step on their toes." He also recommends that we do not change the subject. What our customer is discussing is important to them–let's respect them and their interests.

We must manage our emotions. Some conversations can generate feelings that if displayed, would be counterproductive to getting the sale. Frustration, anger, and fear are just a few to mention that must be controlled. Listening responsively shows the customer that we are fully engaged. Paraphrase, nod, and laugh where appropriate – stay engaged and let them know it!

Our ability to engage **Principle 6: "Every moment counts: be in this moment"** is exemplified by our ability to listen. Our tendency to go off on tangents or focus on our point of view is a conversation energy drain and Principle 6 is energy food. We can use what are called response generators instead of questions to maintain momentum, for example, "tell me more" or "Wow that must be frustrating, go on." These simple comments allow the conversation to take its natural course and enables the prospect to sustain their focus on the topic.

How do we know when we are in a conversation about our client's needs?

Our customers at some point will acknowledge the value in moving from their current state to some future desired state. The drivers for this move will be their desire to increase or decrease good and bad business outcomes. For example, they may say, "I want to increase capacity, reduce waste, grow revenue or reduce cost. They will state this in broad, general terms first and we will need to recognize this language so we can prepare to summarize their needs in a condensed, meaningful way. Our job will be to move the conversation from broad, overarching needs to a specific needs statement. It might sound like this, "So you want to increase capacity, how much, when, and at what cost?

By getting more specific in this way, we drive the conversation in a jointly meaningful direction. What is the budget? What are the specifications? When will the decision be made? What are the absolute 'must haves' for your procurement? What are some desirables beyond the 'must haves' for this procurement, and so forth? We can begin to link benefits and payoffs to the answer to these questions thus preparing our solutions presentation to be clear, concise and effective.

You cannot sell until you can summarize the client's need(s). This is the heartbeat of the sales process and the most critical component to ensure a satisfied customer. In the absence of identifying needs, we are resorting to the oft-used phrase 'feature dumping'. So it is important to know how to ask questions to unearth needs and to know when we are in an active needs-based conversation. Let's remember, the most powerful words a salesperson can say during any sales conversation is, "...you told me that you needed..." When we follow this expression with an accurate summary of the client's needs we are ready to position a solution.

What is our client's sales cycle?

There are obvious times when an opportunity presents itself, for example, at the end of a contract, which is the most common. Or when an existing vendor defaults or performs so poorly and creates pain for the customer that motivates them to look for a change immediately. To respond to these situations, we just need to be known by the customer and well positioned to fill the vacuum.

Needs come from a desire to make a certain business situation better. All successful companies engage in strategic planning. It is the way in which they respond to their business environment, to grow or consolidate to improve business outcomes. In doing so, they engage in a strategic planning process that defines their "go forward actions". The process begins when business leaders think deeply about the future state of their business and they establish a vision for their future. Then they examine their current situation. So, to get from where they are now (current state) to where they want to be (vision or desired state), they set broad goals. Each goal has an action plan to satisfy its intention. Each action plan has tasks, metrics, timetable, budget, responsible stakeholders and an accountability process. The action plan will include the procurement of additional resources, capital equipment and expenditures, vendor down-selection and specification refinement. It is during this activity that the decision is made to buy the products or services you (or your competitor) sell.

How do I know when to move on?

This is perhaps the most difficult judgment call of any professional when the energy has run its course during questioning for needs. We've reached the point where the thicket of objections becomes onerous, the client closes up or just puts a verbal stop to the conversation. We may be certain at this point that there is a latent objection underlying the resistance, but we are unable to unearth it. Admittedly, this can be frustrating.

TIPS: REASONS WHY THE PROSPECT CLOSED UP

- We went off topic
- We ran over time
- We did not see or act on buying or objection signals
- We said something off base or challenged a sensitivity

How do I know when I am on the right track?

Our objective is to learn about their business and understand their needs. So a successful conversation about needs occurs when the prospect or client is acknowledging that they are trying to improve a situation by increasing or decreasing as an aspect of their situation. They are trying to increase revenue, efficiency, profit, customer satisfaction, quality or performance. They may be trying to decrease waste, unused space, or inefficient operations. These are strong clues that you are engaged in the right conversation.

Now with the features of our solution in mind, we are now asking questions that will allow us to best position our product or service to match their need. Questioning in order to isolate the primary needs is what will make us most efficient in communicating our solution while keeping its benefits specific to the main interest of the client.

During a seminar, we brought a willing participant to the front of the room to sell us an iPhone. It was someone that we identified previously that was a very enthusiastic iPhone user. We told them that we are interested in purchasing an iPhone and we wanted them to sell us on it. Well, the unassuming participant then leaps into a tirade about the most popular features of the phone all the while looking for our reaction. He was ready to pounce on any positive signal to a particular feature. After a few minutes, we asked the class if they believed we were sold. Generally there was consensus that there was no sale made.

We then asked the volunteer to dig into our potential needs for the phone by asking why we might want the phone and how we would use it. After a few obvious questions like, "What will you be doing with your phone?", we responded with, "…we are Wedding DJs and, while we want the phone to do all the things a phone normally does, we really want to use it as a backup for all our music so that we won't be left hanging at our gig when/if our computer fails." This changed the conversation completely, and the questions were now more focused on our need to have the device to support our music business. The volunteer was better prepared to sell us the phone by focusing on our primary need.

The class was quite responsive to the example and realized immediately how easy it was to sell us something we already wanted when our needs were known. Conversely, the class made note of how difficult it might be to sell something when the salesperson doesn't work to find out the customer needs and resorts to sharing a feature laundry list instead.

So in our questioning, we are looking for both verbal and non-verbal buying signals. We are also attuned to the client's energy during the conversation. If we sense they are exhibiting more energy in their conversation tone and are more animated with their non-verbal language, then we know that we have arrived at a subject that we want to explore. Remember, we will be looking for these same non-verbal clues after we have presented our solution. This will help us as we prepare to "Bridge the Gap".

Summary for exploring the Gap

We have reviewed the main reason for exploring the gap, the types of questions you can use for your exploration and some keys to get the information you seek in an organized, digestible way. The objective was to uncover the client's need(s) and have the opportunity to successfully link the benefits of our solution to that need. Next, we need to examine all of the deeper benefits, consequences and options that we can reveal to ensure that our solution can be refined and communicated with precision.

STEP 3: BUILD A BRIDGE

Our questioning strategy needs to start at a broad, general level. We call this 'exploring the gap'. When it is time to refine the information we need to construct our solution around their need. Our questions uncover specific information so that our solution can be precisely crafted and stated. We refer to this step in the process as "Building the Bridge".

As we ask the right questions of our clients, we are gathering the information necessary to comfortably explain the most relevant benefits of our product/service. This ability puts us in a better position to make the sale and solidifies the importance of an effective question strategy. Our questioning approach needs to be organized, structured and efficient thus permitting our customers to be organize in their responses. This should save time for both of us.

Our questions flush out important material related to their business challenges and our challenges to help solve them. The questions we ask are likely related to these topics to assemble a more complete landscape of the world around the deal. For example:

- Who is involved in the decision making of the deal? What is/are:
    - Their situation and their plans to improve it?
    - Their needs and how our proposed solution satisfies them?
    - Production delivery details...how much, when, where, who?
    - Specification details...weight, size, speed, or package?
    - The effects our solution has on their customers?

- The obstacles to improving their situation?
- The payoffs for them when improving their situation?
- The consequences of their not improving their situation?
- The impact of selecting our solution on their decision makers?
- Our competition and their approach to this customer?
- Potential objections that might arise?
- The emotional payoff for solving their business problem?

The best approach is to begin by asking general questions. This will start the questioning strategy and our intent should be to move from general questions and general responses to more specific questions and responses. For example, "you said that you want to grow your business over the next few years. What is the specific level of growth you are targeting within the next 18 months?"

The reason we drive for more specific information is to allow us to paint a clear picture of their needs so we can summarize needs, present our solution and close. Specifics allow our prospects to visualize their challenge and our solution. For example:

"You told me that you need to improve inventory turns from 4 to 5 turns per year. Our product will help you achieve that. Here's how."

Sounds better than,

"You said you want to improve inventory turns, we can help. Here's how."

Our customers buy specific solutions because they have specific business challenges, so we need to work for the specifics in our questioning approach. Our questions progress from general to specific to specifications. Knowing how our customers conduct their planning will also help us question in a more structured and organized way. *This planning can take place locally in a buyer's workspace or at the boardroom level.* How do companies make their strategic plans? This is important to know because it is during their strategic planning that our solution may be identified. Most successful companies sequester their executives away for a long week or weekend to conduct their 3–5 year strategy sessions. During these strategic retreats, they will employ tools that identify where they want the company to go and how they would like to get there. The traditional model that most companies use to strategically plan looks similar to this.

- Vision – What is the company striving to accomplish?
- Current State – Where are they now?
- Goals – How they get from 'the now' to 'the future'.
- Action Planning – What specific actions will they take?
    - Timetable – milestones and deadlines for completion of the action steps.
    - Budget – Capital (CapX) v. operations (OpX) expense or budgeted from working capital to achieve goals.
    - Responsible people – who is responsible for implementation of action plans.
    - Resources – People, things, and intangibles needed to complete actions.
    - Accountability and follow through – How will everyone be assured actions are on time, on budget making progress to completion?

If they have truly gone through strategic planning and they have created detailed actions around that plan, it is likely they have created the framework for our solution. There might even be a detailed specification or an initiative to explore available solutions in the works. These will require our efforts to discover.

A large disaster recovery IT firm, well known for hosting data for large institutions where access to stored data is critical for business performance, used their client's strategic planning process to position themselves for success. In the aftermath of 9/11, they flourished as large companies had to demonstrate business continuity as part of their risk management strategy. This company knew that their solution was part of any overall strategic implementation and they positioned themselves around budget and planning cycles to make their move. They even worked with prospects to build the data access, recovery and managed services to design the specification so that they were the only company that could meet it. This company knew the value of questioning around the construct of their clients' strategies. Their sales force would ask questions about business continuity specifications needed to sustain their business in the event of a catastrophic event. Asking for this information early in the process allows for a more effective construct of a solution statement.

We create the highest level of motivation for our customers when we find their true, deep need. Take the following story as an example. A company received a form letter from a large customer asking for a price reduction of 10%. This letter was sent to all their major vendors in an attempt to reduce costs. The demand for a price decrease was offered in exchange for a promise by the customer to 'remember' the good act, especially when it came time to renew the business. Most companies, receiving such a demand letter, would respond with the 'no thanks' letter or offer some unilateral concession. The vendor had 40% of the customer's business for their product group, representing three million in annual sales and they suspected that the competitor, who had the larger portion of business, was considering a price concession to keep their share.

The vendor instead wanted to learn more about what was driving the demand for a price reduction and viewed this more as an opportunity to build relationships and gain market share. They requested a face-to-face meeting with the VP of purchasing, finance, and contracts. During the meeting the vendor asked the customer, "What drivers led up to your request?" The executives in the room were quick to let them know that they needed $99 million in cash to bring their business in line with corporate goals. They were seeking this in the way of price concessions to preserve working capital and reduce the value of their existing inventory. "So it is cash you need, and not necessarily a price concession, right?" This realization was invaluable for the vendor. They countered a few weeks later by offering to purchase the entire customer owned inventory in their product group and lease it back to them. By acquiring their inventory, they were able to write the customer a check for $ 4 million. They also provided a turnkey service enabling the customer to acquire inventory when and where they needed it, upon request. The customer was tentative at first, but then it became apparent that they were receiving 4% toward their cash goal. That was a needle mover. In return, the vendor received 100% of the business and a price increase and a secured, long term agreement.

TIPS FOR ORGANIZING OUR QUESTIONS

- Start with general questions.
- Work toward more specific responses.
- Determine what the customer must have.
- Determine what the customer would also like to have.

Summary for building a bridge

The more effective we are at asking questions to understand the complete situation, the more proficient we will be at closing deals. When we leave the questioning phase of the process and jump too quickly to presenting our solution, we lose focus of where we are in the process and extend the path to the deal. Top salespeople know how to ask good questions because they plan them and know how to use the customer responses to craft a solution that meets or exceed the customers' needs.

STEP 4: BRIDGE THE GAP

We have earned the right to present our solution when we can successfully summarize the client's need. An annual report on the state of American journalism, written by the Pew Research Center, stated that "print advertising fell for a sixth consecutive year in 2012, and not by just a little–it dropped $1.8 billion, or 8.5%, in a slowly improving economy. National advertising is a particular weakness, suggesting that corporations are shifting their advertising dollars to other platforms. Newspapers continue to reduce traditional newsroom staff with smaller expansion on the digital side. A few have also cut print frequency to three times a week. In a symbolic indicator of decline, newspapers are abandoning the grand headquarters buildings that used to help anchor downtowns in favor of smaller, less expensive offices. Those that stay are starting to rent excess space to other businesses". It is evident that our newspaper industry is facing significant challenges to its success and given this fact, how do we explain the unprecedented success of The Daily Record in Dunn, North Carolina? This local newspaper boast a circulation of 112%, which means that more people read the Daily Record than live in the city of Dunn.

Now stop for a moment before reading further and give yourself the opportunity to think about this situation. We challenge you to come up with the right answer before you read on. What could The Daily Record be doing, that every other major newspaper in the United States is not? The answer is names, names, names. This is the Principle 3 in action!

Hoover Adams, the founder of The Daily Record, believed that people read a local newspaper for local news. This sounds simple enough, unfortunately most local newspapers are unable to execute on this simple fact. Most local papers, for example are loaded with national stories and discussions on professional sports teams. To the contrary, if you want to know whose son, in Dunn, has just made the high school football team you'll find that in The Daily Record. If you want to know whose apple pie won first-place at the County Fair, you will find that in The Daily Record. Simply put, if you want to see your name and the name of your friends and family in print you better put aside the USA Today or The News & Observer and get yourself a copy of The Daily Record. Let's think about this, when our name appears in a newspaper, for any reason, how do we react? Yes we buy it, save it and buy more for friends and family. It becomes a novelty.

Principle 6 states, "Every moment counts, be in this moment". The Daily Record, stays in the moment with each of its readers by only discussing what is most important to them. When we engage our future customer, in an effort to communicate how our product or service will deliver on the value they seek, we must only discuss what is most relevant to them and NOTHING ELSE!! So, the key to a successful presentation of our solution, after we have summarized the client need, is to say just enough and no more to get the buyer's commitment. We like to call this 'being surgical' in our solutions' presentation. First we need to summarize the need, so we start the presentation with.

"You told me that you needed to…"

Completing this statement is how we summarize the prospect's needs which is an essential prelude to presenting any solution. Next we just need to communicate how we satisfy those needs through our solution.

Presenting our solution:

Objective: Clearly and concisely sharing only relevant information with our prospect, enabling them to best see the value in our solution.

Tools:

- risk reduction questions for buyers
- solution equation

We accomplish this feat with the use of the Solution Equation. Our customer will gain the "Clarity of Value" as long as we follow the formula. Let's review the formula, step by step.

The Solution Equation

$$\textbf{Clarity of Value} = \frac{\textbf{(Need + Fact + Benefit + Gap Description + Trial Close) X Proof}}{\textbf{Customer Needs}}$$

Our team not only works with salespeople, we also work with buyers, usually in negotiation workshops. Buyers need for us to be clear, concise and relevant. To do so, we have refined a method to meet the buyers need for brevity and clarity. To keep our solution presentation simple and short winded, we offer a simple list of questions to answer. These questions become the construct of communicating your solution presentation. The questions are…

1. What did my client tell me their needs were? (Need)
2. What is my solution called? (Fact)
3. What are some of the features, facts and functionality of my solution? (Fact and Benefit)
4. How will my customer benefit from my solution? (Make a strong link to the customers' need) (Benefit)
5. What specific/identifiable situation will we improve? (Gap Description)

6. Do I have evidence that my solution can work for my customer? (Proof)
7. Who are some of the others I have helped? Testimonials. (Proof)
8. Test our progress with a "trial close"

Here is an example of this model in practice. The company is a relocation service run by a strong boutique company that specializes in moving corporate executives that have just been hired by large firms and need to be moved from one city the next. They are selling to a large manufacturing firm located in Atlanta, GA who is looking for a relocation partner to facilitate a merger that has occurred recently. The clients' needs have been established to…

- make the move seamless for the client and the company
- build a relationship with the executive being moved, and treat them like a VIP
- report progress in a timely way, including issues
- stay within budget established for client move

Since this relocation company can summarize the needs clearly, they are in a good position to present their solution. Here is a strong way for the salesperson to state the solution incorporating our 8 point structure described above.

1 – Summarize the need:
"You told me there is a need to create an executive "VIP" experience as we assist in the relocation of your new executive. You said there is a need for us to be efficient and budget conscious. As well, you need a good process for communicating the progress and any issues. And more

importantly, you want the client to see the quality of their experience with you through the quality of the transition we facilitate. Did I get that right?"

2 – What is my solution called?

Our VIP relocation service satisfies each of your needs.

3 – And, what are some of the features, facts and functionality of my solution?

Here's how it works. First, we review and get your expectations aligned with our process. Then we review your guidelines and policies in detail and maintain the integrity of your process. We learn about the executive and get details of your special requests and/or those of the client. Next, we meet and get to know the executive being moved. Then, engage our resources to match the property with the client, and manage the process for disposition of the property being vacated. All the while, we use our online progress tool to keep you up to date on the progress of the relocation with detailed activities, issues and performance to budget metrics. How does that sound so far?

4 – How will you benefit from my solution? (Make a strong link to the customers' need.)

Through this approach, you will feel the comfort that we support and mirror your quality brand by giving your executive the experience they expect and deserve. And you can relax knowing that you have fingertip control over the progress and spend-to-budget of the move at any moment through your online dashboard access.

5 – What specific/identifiable situation will we improve?
The challenges you have experienced in the past will not be repeated. The discourteous drivers, late pick-ups and mediocre treatment of the executives are a thing of the past.

6 – Do I have evidence that my solution can work for you?
Here are some facts from our prior experience with companies such as yours. Since we measure our client satisfaction, you can see here that we have a 4.8 client satisfaction rating out of a possible score of 5 over the past six years. This is the highest client satisfaction ranking in the industry.

7 – Who are some of the others I have helped? (Testimonials)
I have two letters from current clients that are enjoying the same benefits that you seek and are so satisfied that they took the time to let us know in writing. If you wish, I can put you in touch with them so you can speak to them personally. Can I do that for you?

As you can see, it does not take long to present a solution when you are armed with a clear understanding of their needs. I am sure the relocation company has many other features and functionality to support their service. There is no need to elaborate on those yet. That can be done once the deal is done and you are in the contract negotiation process. Those additional features are sources of value that remind the client of the good decision they have made. And they can be used as bargaining chips at the negotiation table.

8 – Test our progress with a "trial close".
What do you think so far?
How does this sound to you?

TIPS: STEPS TO POSITION OUR PRODUCT TO MEET NEEDS

Step 1: Summarize the customer's needs

Step 2: Present facts, function and features about our company, products and services related only to each customer need

Step 3: Link benefits to needs

Step 4: Be specific about the challenges they currently face that will be addressed by our solution

Step 5: Express proof

Step 6: Present testimonial or success story.

Step 7: Trial close

Forms of Evidence

To make our solutions presentation convincing, we need to offer evidence to support our recommendation. We have found that salespeople intentional about including solid forms of evidence have the most success in converting a presentation to a sale. So let's examine a few of the forms of evidence that are available to us. We have listed just a few options here as a start. As you review, feel free to create additional forms of evidence of your own. .

Demonstrate your product or service

From plant tours to desktop screen views, demonstrations are an effective way to show prospects the quality-conscious and/or user-friendly capability of our solution, in a hands-on way. "A picture is worth a thousand words" may be an overused cliché, but it remains just as true now as it will be when you are demonstrating your benefits.

TIPS TO DELIVERING A SUCCESSFUL DEMONSTRATION...

- Prepare a "screen play" of your demonstration
- Rehearse with your peers and subject manner experts

- Anticipate questions and objections
- Have a back-up plan
- Never allow a prospect to demonstrate your product without you

Telling stories and using examples

Stories are powerful forms of evidence. Telling stories gets the customer's mind working in a visual way. They need to have details that appeal to the senses and emotions of the listener. They should be crafted in such a way to assist the listener with a mind-picture of the incident. So, stay focused and restrict the story's length to a short time frame. Remember, we only have about 90 seconds with someone one-on-one when telling stories before we lose them.

Example: We helped a customer recently achieve a 12% savings over an 18-month timeframe with our solution. They were seeking better use of their inventory space with merchandise that would turn 25% faster. Customers were just not buying the current item in this otherwise popular segment of their offerings. Our solution produced immediate results from the moment it hit the shelf. Our customer was so happy they made the decision to hire us. I believe you would realize a similar benefit.

TIPS FOR TELLING STORIES

- Keep it brief
- Add enough detail that appeals to senses and emotions
- Be sure it's relevant to the point you are making
- End with a summary linking the story to your presentation

Facts and Statistics

Facts are indisputable nuggets of data. The reason they are so effective is that they cannot be challenged. Yet, we so often offer unsupported data as fact when, they are simply our opinions. Gather facts about your product/services and prepared to cite your sources.

This is especially true for statistics, which are a probability over a given data set. We casually offer statistics without citing the source. In our sales workshops, we will often make the statement that "...57.3 percent of all statistics are made up, including this one." It makes the point. Customers understand that we can make numbers tell any story we wish, so use third-party data when available and do not let statistics be the only evidence provided. Remember trust is based on our ability to be credible. So, cite your source and make sure it is a source respected by your prospect or client.

We often know when we are about to hear an opinion because it is precluded with "I think", "I feel", or "I believe". These phrases scream to us that an opinion is coming. People respond to opinions in unpredictable ways. The only opinion that matters belongs to the customer. If the customer has stated an opinion of our products or service, listen to it carefully, ask questions to gain understanding of their position and address it accordingly. If their opinion mirrors ours, confirm it. If their opinion is different from ours, consider using the objection handling process, the NURSE formula, which we will discuss in **Section 5, Walk the Bridge**.

Visual Aids and Marketing Print Material (Collateral)

Visual aids are effective, widely used forms of evidence. Marketing departments often produce these materials to be used in concert with presenting our products/services to prospective customers, and it is prudent for us to know what's in them. If correctly done, they are also created with the intent to spread a brand message that needs to be repeated in our presentations to become effective.

PowerPoint or Prezi presentations are a form of visual aid, and for the more complex sale, an essential part of any sales cycle. We give them when we are describing our company's capabilities as well as when we are offering a solution. Just remember that when we are presenting, using these tools, we are delivering the message, not the slides. We have seen these presentations given in a dark room without the ability to see anyone's face. The lights go out and we begin with our 141-slide deck attempting to sell our company and ourselves. We might as well serve two sleeping pills and a glass of warm milk.

TIPS FOR USING VISUALS AIDS AND PRODUCT COLLATERAL

- Use them when you need them, then move them away.
- Know what is in them and what work was done to create them.
- Know the source of any supporting information.
- Be intentional about when you are going to reveal them.

Summary for Bridging the Gap

Presenting solutions is easy when we remember the following:

- Know the customer's need(s).
- Use the 7 question template.
- Stay concise in our delivery.
- Link the features and benefits to the customer's needs.
- Have a few strong forms of evidence to convince the prospect.
- Present one point at a time.
- Trial close after each point for confirmation of understanding and alignment.
- Use the value equation to ensure we have all the elements of a cohesive solutions presentation and it is knitted together in such a way as to set the table for your customer's commitment.

STEP 5: WALK THE BRIDGE

Creating Motivation in Preparation for the Close

"There's a fire. Quick, get the gasoline!"

We sometimes have the privilege of traveling with salespeople to observe them as they conduct their sales calls. We then go into the training room where they learn the art of consulting vs. selling. We observe them again following the training to see the transformation. On one occasion, we traveled with such a salesperson, Jeanne, who worked for a food brokerage company. Her usual sales call involved carrying a cooler of food samples to large retail restaurants to entice the owner/manager to purchase these items through their normal distribution channel. As a broker, she was compensated by the volume of sales that were generated through the distributor.

One afternoon, Jeanne traveled to a large retail seafood establishment on the east coast. The proprietor, Robert "Bob", greeted Jeanne as she entered and asked, "What's new?" She said "…plenty," and proceeded to empty her cooler on a table in the lounge. "I have fried pickles, chicken nuggets, potato wedges and key lime tarts." Bob retorted, "Great! Lets' cook them up and serve some to the folks at the bar and a few of the staff, and if they like them, I'll order some." After the tasting, Bob immediately stated that he would place an order for the nuggets and tarts but nothing else. As we started our trip back to Jeanne's office we asked, "How do you think the call went?" "Great, he's going to order some." she said.

As we spent time in the classroom learning a more consultative way to engage a customer, we witnessed the light bulbs brighten as Jeanne began to embrace the approach. Our next visit to Bob's restaurant was quite different. As she entered the restaurant, Bob said, "Hey Jeanne, what's new?" Jeanne returned, "I was just going to ask you the same question. What are you trying to do to grow your business?" Bob countered, "Glad you asked, I want to grow my lounge business. Our weekend business is good thanks to sports fans and tourists. But the weekday nights are lean and I wanted to create some theme nights to bring locals in. You know, trivia, poker, karaoke nights." Jeanne listened and took note. Rather than immediately chiming in, she asked another question. "What will that do for your business if you are able to create that type of traffic?" Bob was quick to respond, "I can hire a manager, and get a life. My wife and I have property on a lake and have not been able to build since we bought it five years ago. It would be a dream come true for us if we were able to build on it and spend some time there." Jeanne was quick to empathize. "That sounds like a wonderful goal. And, I have some ideas for your special nights. We can create a menu of snacks and small plates to go with the themes, you know, poker 'chips' and karaoke 'kabobs'." Bob was very enthused and their brainstorming conversation lasted more than an hour.

On the way back to Jeanne's office, we stopped at a hardware store where she bought an attractive 'welcome' mat. Back in her office, she placed it in an express mail container addressed to Bob with a note, "Here is the 1st installment on that home on the lake. Lets' get to work and make it happen." Needless to say Bob and Jeanne have been collaborating for years now and they both have benefited from increased business.

Learning a sales process and adhering to it is vital but not a be-all-end-all. There is an art form to selling and it is most evident near the end of a sales process. How do we know when it is time to close? Yes, we are looking for the proverbial buying signals. You know, those verbal and non-verbal cues that indicate a strong buying interest with a preclusion to complete the transaction.

Reading Buying Signals

We have emphasized throughout this book that the sales process is not about us, it is about the prospective customer. Recognizing this fact should motivate us to always focus on them. When we are presenting our solution, the need to understand the disposition of our prospect is essential and paying attention to their body language will help in this effort.

Most of us can distinguish positive verbal and non-verbal signals because our ability to do so has been hard-wired in us since infancy. We would like to reinforce that wiring by reviewing some contrasting signals or 'tells' to look for when determining the level of interest of our prospect. These signals are invitations to either advance the sale or peel back underlying concerns. Here are some lists of positive verbal and non-verbal signals that are strong indicators of interest.

Positive Verbal signals

- Repeated agreement with our statements.
- Positive responses to trial closes.
- Questions for deeper understanding.
- Asking us to repeat or clarify a benefit.
- Offers humor (not sarcasm or cynicism) or laughter.
- Offers additional options or modifies solution.
- Tries to negotiate terms or specifications.

Positive non-verbal signals

- Open arms
- Eyes and head up
- Hands and feet facing toward us
- Lips slightly open
- Palms facing up when talking
- Smiling, head nodding up and down
- Head tilted slightly sideways

The negative verbal and non-verbal signals denote an underlying objection or an indication that the buyer has not been totally honest about their interest or their buying process. It is best to address these signals sooner than later. And, it is best to take a head-on approach and ask directly about any hesitancy. A consultant's code is to make sure that you do not allow your customer to make a mistake. This should be our motive to press for clarity around their hesitation as indicated by these behaviors.

Negative verbal signals

- Criticizes comments we have made or our communication style ("You're not listening to me.")
- Expresses forms of doubt. ("I'm not sure that applies to us.")
- Sighing, grunting or a 'low frequency hum-burst'.
- Smacking lips.
- Frequent use of the words "...yes, but."

Negative Non-verbal signals

- Brow lowered
- Arms folded, closed body position
- Pursed or close mouth and lips
- Scowl
- Rapid eye movement
- Head moving side to side
- Hands touching or rubbing their face, ears, nose, forehead or back of head
- Fingers covering the mouth
- Head straight and still
- Eyes looking down or an indirect glare
- Eye glasses on lower bridge of nose

What happens when the customer's buying signals are speaking hesitation, doubt or negativity? This must be dealt with for the sale to progress. These signals are often subtle, but most often present themselves in the form of an objection. Learning how to handle objections will help to define us as a professional salesperson. It is the most valuable opportunity to conduct a dynamic conversation in this moment because we are managing potential conflict that is accompanied by emotion.

Handling Objections

Objections are like the wild card in the sales conversation. It is the part where we seem to lose or relinquish control to the prospect. There is usually resistance and emotions that accompany the objection. How we respond to that objection will define us as a professional. This is not the time to dither or wither. These are basic tenets to keep in mind while handling an objection.

- Find points of agreement with the customer early in the of handling their objection
- Help the customer feel comfortable that they are not alone in their concern and we will alleviate this concern together
- Get all customer objections on the table before addressing any of them

Before we can discuss how to effectively handle a customer objection, we must be very clear on the definition of a valid objection. We often look at an objection as a roadblock to moving the sales process forward, but it is exactly the opposite. A genuine objection is simply a customer request for more information. They need clarity to better understand the value our product/service will provide them.

Simple exercise: If you have sold your current product or service for at least 12 months, stop and think for a moment. How many objections have you heard within the last 30 days that you never heard before? We are willing to bet the answer is zero.

We have asked this question to groups as few as five and as many as two hundred and the most we have ever seen is maybe one person raise their hand. Why is this the case? What does this tell us? The answer is obvious. If we have been selling our chosen product or service for at least 12 months, we have heard every objection we are likely to hear. This very point should be a source of immense excitement!

When I (Andre) began my selling as a stockbroker trainee my largest apprehension was what to do when the client said no. How many of us have felt nervous, anxious, frustrated or angry, at the presence of a customer objection? Let me share this story with you and I promise, from this point forward, you will take a giant step toward feeling only confidence when faced with a customer objection.

One day while attempting to close a sale with a prospective client, the client said to me "Andre I do not have enough money". I turned to my trainer, covered the phone, and mouthed the words "he says he does not have enough money". My trainer said "Andre look at the book". On my desk like on many others, there was a three ring binder labeled — OBJECTIONS. This book had several dividers, one of which was labeled NOT ENOUGH MONEY. I turned to that page and read the following words, "Mr. Customer, I understand."

Next the prospective customer said, "Andre that sounds fine, but I cannot make this decision without speaking first to my business partner." I covered the phone, turned to my trainer and mouthed the words, "...he wants to speak with his business partner." My trainer repeated, "Look at the book!" Again there was a divider labeled, BUSINESS PARTNER, which I eagerly read. By the third objection, I was a "pro", not at handling objections, but at finding the appropriate section in the three-ring binder. By the way, I did close that sale.

Our lesson is this — there is no need to feel anything less than confident when handling an objection, because we have heard them all before. Prepare, prepare, prepare and meet every objection with a smile. We should immediately make note of every objection we have ever heard in addition to every objection our peers have ever heard and start to create solid answers for these objections. We should update this list as often as necessary to maintain our confidence that there is no objection a customer could share, for which, we don't have a concise and convincing answer. We must have answers that will help our customers feel comfortable assuming the risk to do business with us. We must always remember if we are asking a prospect to change the current way of doing business, they are assuming all the risk. They are risking a lot, for example, their operational productivity and efficiency, business revenue and income, corporate/personal reputation and brand just to name a few. If something goes wrong, after making this decision, they will likely pay a price. We on the other hand, in most cases, have only risked a little of our time. We must do all we can to minimize the customer's risk by fully understanding what they need, providing an exceptionally valuable/appropriate solution then accurately setting the customer's expectations for results.

Objections have the ability to cause damage to the warm relationship we are developing. If this happens, we want to do all we can to nurse this relationship back to health.

Now let's examine the process of handling an objection using the **NURSE** formula.

Step 1: Neutralize
Step 2: Uncover
Step 3: Ratify

Step 4: Satisfy
Step 5: Engage

Yes that's right, we figuratively nurse our objections back to health. Here is how the formula works.

Neutralize

Most objections that we receive are based upon our customer's reality, either driven by their past experiences, current perception or lagging doubt. These objections are also emotionally charged – so beware. We are well served to validate the objection and the emotions involved. We call this neutralizing the objection. Common objections often revolve around issues of price, quality, customer service, incumbent loyalty or a poor past experience with our product/service. We will deal with each one of these and more in **Step 4, Satisfy**.

When we neutralize, we are just stating their concern in such a way as to validate without agreeing or disagreeing with what they have said. We commonly recommend words such as…

- "I'm glad you brought that up."
- "I understand that you want to make the best decision for your business"

PRICE:

- "I understand that it is important that you make the best investment for your business."
- "I see you want to make sure you are getting the best value."

QUALITY – INCUMBANT LOYALTY

- "I understand it is important that your vendor be able to meet all of your needs."

- "I understand it is important that you are comfortable with your vendor."

CUSTOMER SERVICE

- "Sounds like you demand the best possible service to support your product choice."

If the customer has had a previously poor experience with us, it is important that our response is passionate. Our response should be crisp and needs to match the emotional energy to which the objection is delivered. For example, "Wow, we need to deal with this right away to assure you never have an experience like that with us again." The key is to let them know we care about their issue and we intend to work through it with them. We believe it's important to create the feeling that we are going to be thinking partners with our customers. We might say something like the following, "Let's work together on this 'thing' that concerns you."

Uncover

When an objection is delivered, it often comes with very little information. It is usually a sound bite, with a sharp edge. "Your price is too high." When we hear one such as this, we have a choice. We can assume that we know what they mean and respond, or we can uncover how they reached that conclusion. The safe ground is to uncover the basis for their objection. This is the time to be naturally curious. We now combine the neutralizing statement with a series of questions to find out what stands behind the objection.

Customer: "Your price is too high"
Salesperson (neutralize): "Ok, I see. You want to make sure you're getting the best value."

Salesperson: "What are you comparing our price with at this point?"
Customer: "Both of your competitors have come in with lower prices for similar products."
Salesperson: "Are we comparing similar features, applications and functionality?"

You see where we are going with this? Now we can begin the work of developing our response with a more thorough understanding of their concern. How long do we ask questions? Well, it depends on the type of objection. Some are more complex than others and require some time to uncover the totality of their objection. While we have begun the work of resolving this objection by uncovering, we still have some steps to take to complete the task.

Ratify

Everyone wants to feel heard and understood. We also want to deal with professional people who are interested in helping us make good decisions. The art of ratifying what someone has said during a discussion achieves these aims. Ratifying involves summarizing what the person said with the purpose of validating our understanding and asking permission to satisfy the concern.

We are ratifying their answers to our questions and some insights that have come up during the discussion. Confirming what the prospect has said gives a powerful boost to our credibility as an empathetic listener. This type of validation during a conversation is a hidden secret of successful sales professionals and should not be ignored. Ratifying what we have heard may sound something like this:

"So, I heard you say that you want the best value and our price, while having a higher sticker value, represents a quality upgrade

to your current system and will give you a better return due to efficiencies. Did I get that right?"

There are many advantages to making these kinds of statements. For one thing, it allows us to control the conversation. And, if the subject has some associated negative emotions, it allows us to remove the barbs by restating what they said in a more positive way.

We also want to ratify that we don't have any other objections face us downstream. This is a good time to get them all on the table. Just ask, "…besides your concern about the performance of our solution, is there anything else standing in the way of us moving forward?

Their response will tell you a lot. If they respond that this is the only objection, then all you have to do is satisfy and engage. If they say, "…there is something else", then you may be right to assume that the next objection is the 'real' objection. Go back to the "Neutralize" step and just follow the NURSE formula to handle that objection.

Satisfy

Once we feel we have a good understanding of what is behind the objection and we have a good approach to resolve it, we are ready to satisfy their need for resolving the objection. How do we communicate our solution? Easy, just as we did when we presented our solution in the first place; by answering the same series of solutions' questions for our objection, we can craft language that satisfies it. After summarizing the objection, ask the following.

1. What is our remedy?
2. How does it work?
3. What will it do for you?
4. Can you prove it?

Don't forget to ratify the 'satisfy' or X.

Let's look at an example that uses answers to the questions to satisfy an objection that raises concerns about the security of a cloud based managed enterprise service. The client is hesitant to move from their hardware based data management to the cloud.

1. You told me that you were concerned about the security of our enterprise cloud management solution for your Internet retail operation.
2. Our cloud based data service
3. ...is the most secure system available today. Our hardware has three levels of security that prevents unwanted intrusion and interruption.
4. What this means to you is that your data will always be available, but only to you for your business purposes.
5. We currently use this system in over 24 banks and have protected their clients 'data in the cloud' for over 5 years without losing business continuity.
6. We would like to see you realize similar benefits. Did that answer your concern about the security of your data?

Engage

This is the step where we bring the conversation about the objection back to the conversation about the sale. At this point, we need some linking language to jump back into the sales process. We call this "ratify-the-satisfy". We just need the customer's validation that the objection has been handled completely. We are looking for a strong affirmation and once received we can jump back in to where we left off in the sales process.

There are times when we solve the objection only to find that it is the final act before closing. We notice that the buyer has changed their attitude and the buying signals have reversed from tentative to strong. This may be a good time to setup the close.

TIPS FOR HANDLING OBJECTIONS

- Partner with your prospect to work on their objection together.
- Be curious about what is behind the objection.
- Validate that it was resolved.
- Ask, "Besides this concern, is there anything else?"

There are times when the hesitation signals just mean that the prospect has not been emotionally moved enough to act on a purchasing decision. The behaviors may not singularly be a response to an objection, but could be a need for more convincing to bolster the 'feeling' that a buying decision in your favor is a good decision. There are ways to strengthen the emotional appeal. We just need to add some motivation.

The hardest objections to handle are those where you agree with your client. We telegraph that doubt to our client through non-verbal 'tells' which hinder our progress. "Your price is too high," they might say. If you also believe that what the customer just said is true, you will struggle to defend your price. So first, we need to sell ourselves on all the elements and sources of value that make up our price. Believe in them and defend them with an unshakable attitude.

Create the wave...then surf it!

Closing the sale is a significant moment for any salesperson. Some of us know when we are in that moment to ask for the sale and are spring-loaded to take advantage. The key to closing is timing, just like in surfing where the positioning, paddling and one-swift-movement at the crest of the wave is rewarded by a euphoric ride into shore.

Yet, those clues are not always obvious. What if we told you that we could create our own wave, our own environment to gain commitment and incite the strongest buying signal from our prospect? The key to this treasure is to verbalize a mind-picture of the prospect enjoying the benefits of your solution describe what their world might look like a year from now, or next month. Essential to making this effective is to be sure that the picture is in fact a true representation of their most significant benefit. This is not the time to be hokey or patronizing. Keep it real and be sincere. If you nail it, when you ask the question, "…do you see that picture as well? Their response will tell you to proceed or that there are still some objections that need to be addressed.

A car salesperson was working with Jeff, a dad purchasing his daughter's first car. He was extremely concerned about her safety and after several conversations with the salesperson, he still procrastinated on making the decision to buy. The final conversation sounded like this:

Salesman: "Jeff, I just want to make sure I understand your most pressing concern, you still want to make sure that we place Emily in the safest car we can, right?"
Jeff: "Absolutely!"
Salesman: "Fine. This car is top-rated for accident safety and survivability. This is why I recommended the following vehicle." The salesman then shared many of the car's safety facts and statistics with Jeff.
Salesman: "Jeff, picture this, you are standing in the middle of Cobb Parkway and Windy Hill Rd. You see car parts and engine oil all over the road and as you look into the driver's side window of a badly damaged car, you see your daughter sitting behind the wheel and she is smiling at you. Once you see that smile, you are immediately relieved because you realize she is just fine. Now of course, we don't want anything to happen to Emily,

but if she should find herself in this unfortunate situation, that smile, the feeling of knowing she is ok, this is the result you are looking for from this car purchase, isn't it?"

Jeff: "Yes I am."

Salesman: "Fine, then let's make that happen, this is the car for Emily, let's put her in it today."

The car was sold because the salesperson helped Jeff picture himself getting the result he desired. The sales process is designed to complement the customer's buying process. It leads the prospect from a place of vagueness and confusion to a place of clarity and commitment. If done correctly, the prospect is ready to buy when you are ready to close. This doesn't always happen. Our statement, "Create your own wave, and surf it," suggests that we can create the moment that brings the prospect to a point of purchase, willingly. This is done by expressing a visual scenario of the prospect enjoying the benefits of our solution. Identify a relevant time in the future and help the client envision their circumstances improving by adopting our solution. This mind-picture is most effective when it is built around the strongest need that the client has expressed and is as close to their possible reality as possible. In the example above, the intersection discussed was on the route Emily drives daily to go to school and is well known in the area for having accidents. Emily being in the middle of that intersection was easily envisioned by the customer.

Summary for Walking the Bridge

Walking the bridge is the conversation we have with client or prospect after we have presented our solution. This is where we convince the buyer to move ahead with the proposition. It may also be a time for handling resistance, which come in the form of objections. We have given you the structure, process, examples and the motivation to conduct this part of the sales process with vigor and precision. We invite you to incorporate this element into your successful sales conversations.

STEP 6: CLOSE THE GAP

"Closing the sales is actually walking through an open door."

Can I wrap that up for you? How will you be paying? Are you ready to talk financing? Words like these are being used by millions of salespeople at this moment while you are reading this page. Sales are being made and deals are closing all the time. Given where we are in the discussion of the sales process, it's now time for you to ask the same types of questions.

The way in which we ask the questions is dependent upon the complexity of the sale, timing, gut feelings, buying signals and the state of the relationship with the customer. Given so many variables, let's look a multitude of closing options. Some of these closing methods are used alone, some are used together, but all are powerful!

The Closing Toolbox

If we looked into a workman's toolbox, why would we feel uncomfortable if we only saw a single hammer? It is simply because we know that a good workman has a myriad of tools for the different tasks at hand. In the same way, a sales professional must have different tools to close a sale or at least move the sales process forward. Some of our closes will be simply for the purpose of checking the customer's temperature; others will be for the purpose of gaining the customer's commitment. We check the customer's temperature with "Trial Closes" and we ask for commitment with "Completion Closes". Let's take a look at each.

Trial Closes: The Yes, Yes, Yes Close

Trial closes are our surgical tools. If done correctly, they should have been used throughout the sales process and have given the prospect adequate practice at saying "yes". So, we need to be mindful to pose the questions in a positive way that will garner a 'yes' response.

Early in the sales process, we used trial questions as levers to change the subject or continue the discussion. As the process matured, we used them to ensure the prospect is on the same page and their question or objections are being complete answered. They sounded like…

"Did I get that right?"
"Did we answer your question to your satisfaction?"

When we approach the end of the sales process, trial closes become more important as we are checking in to ensure that our final question generates a positive response. They become more deliberate and well crafted. Here are some 'final stage' trial closes to consider.

Opinions Count Trial Close

This is an effective trial close to consider. Simply say, "In your opinion, will this solution solve / help in the following situation?" This way, it's simply an opinion. If the customer says no, we can simply discuss our differences of opinion. This becomes a very strong consultative discussion on the merits of the situation and our prospective opinions on those merits.

Validate the Value Trial Close

This trial close is really purposeful in testing the strongest possible consideration of the deal. Whatever the concern, this question will work. It sounds similar to either of these examples. "Does that seem like a good value to you?" Can you see the quality improvement from this feature?"

Ask For: The Objection Trial Close

If we haven't received any objection at this point in the sales process, but we suspect that they exist, we may want to conduct an assessment. Just ask, "Do you see any obstacles at this point?" We understand that many salespeople are opposed to asking for points that could block progress. However, if we have built a strong enough relationship thus far, you have earned the right to ask for some transparency. Remember, the best time to handle an objection is before it comes up.

Completion Closes: 15 Different Ways to Close (Including Combination Closes)

We have always considered ourselves a collector of closes at Sales Universe and have provided you with a "best of" list. Some of these closing styles work in isolation but many work in tandem to bring the decision-maker to a commitment. The success of these closes will indicate the strength of both our customer rapport and needs assessment.

Be sure to compliment what we say with congruent body language. Nod the head up and down affirmatively. Smile and make sure your body language is open. Square your shoulders to the other person, whether seated or standing. Keep your hands free of any objects that could cause a distraction. Your feet are pointed toward the prospect and your eyes are fixed on theirs in a gentle natural way. Then ask your question and wait, let silence be your ally at this point.

Direct Method

Just ask for it. The key is to say it confidently and concisely. There are many ways to accomplish this type of close. We suggest that you use your own style when asking directly for the close. Can I say we have a deal? This is the final close-ended question. Silence and positive body language are our best friends during this moment. Once we deliver our direct statement, while nodding our head, just wait and let silence do the heavy lifting. Maintain eye contact and a positive facial expression. Relax and wait. Be mindful that in only rare instances does the prospect say "I'll take it!" without us asking for it. This is the trap too many salespeople fall into. They hesitate when asking for the close or do so without the confidence that supports the direct question.

Bear in mind that the responses could be varied and we need to be prepared for each, especially the "yes" response. We address the "acting on the response" later in this chapter, so pay special attention there.

Indirect Method

An indirect close might sound like this: "So what is the process to move the deal along from here?" Or, "Do we need to bring your contracts or lawyer in at this point to negotiate the finer terms?"

As you see, the indirect close usually has something to do with the process of bringing the business in or formalizing the agreement. Should you receive a positive response here you can follow with a direct method such as one we just covered or the next steps method.

Next Steps (Assume the sale)

How often have we found ourselves in the position of the buyer when talking with a salesperson and that salesperson continues to talk even when we are ready to buy and move on? We stand there saying to ourselves "I'm ready, what do I need to do next?" When the presentation is done effectively, more times than not, the sale is already made. We simply assume the customer feels the same way and we say, "The next step in our process is…" This is used when strong buying signals are present and it may be used in tandem with the indirect method where you ask a question that relates to delivery, payment or order process and then state what happens next. Again, be sure to know the process that follows the closing, for example, getting the orders or contracts secured, getting delivery details, logistics, etc. Mostly, be secure, concise and confident in the explanation of the next steps so that there is doubt after the sale. The Next Steps can be in tandem with other closes, as needed, to create a commitment. If we are getting resistance in Next Steps, try using the Opportunity Method or summarize the benefits to position the close again.

Opportunity Method

This is an effective method when used in conjunction with, or as a fall back to, another method. If our direct method did not work, then we can give them a greater sense of urgency by suggesting that they can take advantage of an expiring offer or temporarily available inventory. It sounds like this, "I see you are hesitant...this is the perfect time to move forward because I happen to know that pricing will be changing after the end of the month."

We hear this method used all the time, we just may not recognize it for what it is. Words like "for a limited time only", or "…while they last," are actually opportunity methods to close and effectively create a sense of urgency as it places time or availability limits on the opportunity encouraging a quick transaction or decision.

This is not a method with which we would want to lead, because we have taken away our 'soft place to fall' should they say no or we get some resistance. If appropriate for our business, we should have an opportunity offer available before we present our solution, if our intent is to close the business. This is simply a good practice.

Summarize the Benefits

We might call this type of close "3rd Tier" because it is used after a Direct Method attempt and perhaps an Opportunity Method attempt did not produce the acknowledgement to proceed. Be sure to stay organized and link benefits to their needs, explicitly. We may at this point also want to add an additional feature to change up the conversation.

In summarizing the benefits, we should use the same words that were presented in our solution conversation. Starting with "you told me that you needed", to remind them of their original reason for purchasing and then summarizing the benefits again. This is usually followed with a Trial Close, then a Direct Close or Next Steps Method.

Be careful here. By just repeating what we said earlier, we risk becoming "Charlie Brown's teacher", the mumbling voice in the background, making no progress towards the sale. So change it up and be assertive, passionate, and enthusiastic without being overly aggressive.

Options Method

Sometimes we have a strong buyer/prospect that needs strong involvement at this phase of the buying process. Options give them a choice and are usually positioned in such a way as to allow for a choice between two different products/service groups that have different cost and quality factors. Or, we may have options that would allow for more favorable terms such as delivery, support services, warranty or purchase/ lease arrangements. It might sound like this:

> "We have two directions to consider. You can take delivery of Product 1 at $100 now and save $10. Or we can deliver Product 2 next month and take advantage of its higher quality and save $ 25 over the course of 12 months. Which do you prefer?

We must use our own judgment when deciding to offer all of our options at once or phase them in to manage any objections that may surface later. We can always present them one at a time and phase the offerings to match a client's interest and need. A client might resist a purchase price that exceeds their budget but be open to a lease arrangement that would fit better into their cost structure. Preplan how you would like to present options and know that we are improving our chances of closing in doing so. We like presenting options because "NO" will never be one of their choices.

Alternate Choice Close

Just like the Options Method, we have another solution teed up for the occasion when we are getting strong resistance from our first offering. We strongly recommend having this close ready to go in most situations. It does not have to be a dramatic change. It could simply be a change in delivery or payment terms that might entice the buyer to jump. Just be sure that it is an alternative that would be important to the prospect, which we uncovered during the "Exploring the Gap" phase of the process.

Weighing Method (pluses and minuses)

The Weighing Method is another 3rd Tier close and is best used when other more direct methods have not yielded an affirmative response. The prospect's hesitance may be due to some confusion over how the benefits link to the features of our solution. Thus a logical presentation of the advantages and disadvantages of the decision might provide clarity and a logical case to proceed. The method requires us to list all the advantages on one side of the page and the disadvantages on the other. The goal is then to reduce or eliminate the disadvantages. Or better yet, to convert the disadvantages to advantages. "This negative is actually the very reason why we should move forward with this offer." Just as we emphasized in the section that dealt with communicating our solution, always state benefits to their stated needs.

The conversation is best implemented by taking a legal pad, drawing a line down the middle and labeling one side "advantages" and other side "concerns". Start listing the advantages and have a robust discussion on each point. Gain agreement that these points are actually advantages to the customer and ask if any questions exist about each point before moving to the next. Address any issues that arise when handling the objections process (the NURSE formula). Once the list of advantages is complete, ask the prospect "now what concerns do you have?" Say nothing else. If they are unable to generate a list as robust as the "advantages" list we say, "It looks like the pros out-weigh the cons, let's move forward."

This method is not for the disorganized or the faint of heart. Please practice this one before engaging in its use. Once we have finished delivering the Weighing Method be sure to create the motivation to buy now with an affirmation that the decision is a good one.

Consequence Close

This is a 2nd or 3[d] Tier close and should be used when other more direct methods have not yielded a closed deal. The way it works is to remind the prospect of the consequence of not taking action to save money or improve quality. During the questioning phase of our conversations, we asked the prospect to identify what would happen if they accepted the status quo or missed the opportunity to take advantage of a stronger valued or higher quality solution. Hopefully, earlier in the process, we also asked, what would be the consequences of not filling their need gap with the right solution?

Businesses make decisions every day to avoid consequences. They consolidate operations, change vendors, give discounts or announce a sale price to incentivize their customers. All of this is done to avoid losing business, losing money or missing opportunities.

We believe buyers make the decision to purchase based on the enjoyment of potential benefits, and make decisions to <u>buy now</u> to avoid a consequence. This method is very effective in creating a greater sense of urgency with our buyer. A word of caution — focusing on consequences means that we are asking our customer to maintain a negative frame of mind. We should be prepared to back up our statements with a positive, emotion-based comment directly after they acknowledge the consequence with a strong buying signal. A Consequence Close might sound something like this:

> *"I remember when you told me that changing to this more efficient system would represent a savings of $100K over your current system. And these savings could be rolled into expansion of your commercial channel. I know you don't want to miss one month of these savings, wouldn't you like to take advantage of that savings sooner rather than later?"*

Colombo Close

For those of us familiar with this vintage TV character, here is a method to use in the appropriate situation. Colombo was a homicide detective. He was a very unassuming fellow and would intentionally ask benign questions of his suspects. When finished, he would close his notebook and say, "Well I believe I have what I need for now, take one step toward the door and then say, oh yes, and there is this one more thing." That was the clincher. The suspect had already relaxed in the moment thinking they were off the hook. That one more thing was the impact question that established guilt or innocence. We would rather use this when closing a negotiation as a strong move at the table to exact an important deliverable for the deal, but it can work as an effective close when the element of surprise would exact a positive response.

Puppy dog close (Trial Method)

We have to mention this one or we would not have sales-street credibility or be known as the closing kings. If you haven't heard of this one, you will recognize it anyway. Go to the pet store and hold a puppy or a friendly, purring cat in your arms. Don't be surprised if the store clerk offers this when you resist buying. "Well, you can always take it home for the weekend, and bring it back Monday if you are not happy." No one ever brings the pet back.

Whether you realize it or not, we see this close just about everywhere. "Try it first for 30 days and if you are not satisfied just return it for a full refund." If you can adapt your business to use this close it is an excellent way to gain an unpretentious commitment.

Concession Close

Often during a selling situation, a customer will ask for some sort of a concession. When the customer asks for a concession and we are willing to provide that concession, we should never do so without asking for something in return, and what we ask for is the sale. So we simply say "Mr. Customer if I can take care of this concession, can we close this deal today?"

Something for Nothing Close

Late-night TV, infomercials are great examples of the Something-for-Nothing close. They consistently say, "If you buy today, we will also throw in this free X, Y, or Z." This is our opportunity to share the same thing with our clients. Simply tell your client that if they buy today, we have a free value-offering that we can throw into the deal to make it more enticing. Everyone loves to feel like they got a deal.

Level With Me Close

This is our opportunity to ask our customer for a hidden objection. If we attempt to close and a customer says no, we simply ask, "Would you mind leveling with me — have I failed in some way to show you the value of the solution? If they say yes, we can continue to question the customer on where the "fog" exists. This is an opportunity to continue with our questioning strategy. If they say no, they do see the value, we can simply go ahead and attempt another close or question as to why they're reluctant to make the deal today.

Closing Combinations

<u>Completion Closes 1st Tier</u>

These are the closes that we use in isolation. They are…

- Direct Method
- Options Method
- Colombo Close
- Next Steps

These closes have been described in some detail already and may not need to be addressed further. Most often we will be faced with some resistance at closing and combinations of completion closes will be the needed approach. Become comfortable with using these combinations to ensure that all the time invested to this point will be rewarded.

<u>Combination Closes 2nd Tier</u>

Knowing our customer is key to the proper use of these combinations. We may have already assumed that a Direct Close will not resonate with this prospect. And so, we have intentionally planned to use a combination of closes for this deal. Bravo. It is a smart play to plan our close ahead rather than just blindly starting with a Direct Close and seeing where it goes. Here are some combinations that have proven to be effective when used together. They are…

- Indirect Close + Next Steps
- Direct Close + Opportunity Close
- Direct Close + Alternative Choice Close

An Indirect Close is a Trial Close involving activities that surround the close to test the depth of interest in moving forward. "When is a good day for the delivery of the unit, Tuesday or Thursday?" If you receive a "Thursday" then you can proceed with the next steps with confidence. By the way, this can also be considered an Alternate Choice Close because we have assumed the close and now they have the choice of delivery on Tuesday or Thursday.

A Direct Close that finds resistance lends itself nicely to an Opportunity Close. "Can we get the order placed now?" "Oh, you're not certain now is the best time?" "I just wanted to remind you that we have a limited inventory of this particular item available now, and when we run out, we won't have any available for another 90 days. I say we take advantage of this surplus opportunity now. Do you agree?" You will want to have that strategy planned in advance in the event your Direct Close finds a barrier.

A Direct Close with an Alternative Choice is an excellent strategy to help navigate obstacles, when planned ahead. For a resistance response you could say, "We can offer the same solution as a lease-purchase option that will save you some working capital. Utilizing this option, you will be able move forward with your expansion. Can we get started with this alternative now?"

Common Ground Closes 3rd Tier

When the prior methods have not yielded a strong response to move forward or move on, then a 3rd Tier close could be just the remedy. We use these to bring the decision to the altar. The 3rd Tier closes are…

- Summarize the Benefits
- Ask For the Objection
- Consequence Close

Sometimes the stress of the moment requires clarity and the 'Summarize the Benefits Close guides the discussion to the high ground that sets up the close. If we feel a latent objection is at the heart of their resistance, invite it. Once satisfied, we will find the path to close has gotten easier. People make decisions based on benefits and payoffs. They make decisions *with urgency* to avoid a consequence. The 'Consequence Close is a good way to create urgency which could yield an immediate positive response.

Desperation Closes 4th Tier

As Winston Churchill once said "Never, Never, Never give up!" These closes permit us to keep the deal alive when nothing else has worked. One of the first principles of being a consultant is, "…never let your client make a mistake", therefore since we are convinced that our solution will put them in a better position, let's do our best to help them make the right decision.

- Weighing Method
- Level with Me
- Puppy Dog Close

Remember to practice the Weighing Method so that it is conducted in a smooth way, without bobbles. Since we have rehearsed, we can fill in the pluses and minuses for them until they begin adding their own, assuming they do. The Level with Me close is a plea for transparency, an invitation to be real in the room. We are forcing a yes or a no, so be prepared for either. We just need to know whether to keep this person in the pipeline or move on. The Puppy Dog Close is really just a trial of our product for a specific time. It is very important to be clear on the timeframe. Make sure your client knows that at the end of the trial period they will be faced with a decision to purchase or return the product.

Affirming The Decision to Avoid Buyer's Remorse

Professional salespeople affirm the sale after the close in order to reassure the purchaser that they have made the right decision. This is done because buyer's remorse is real. It's not overwhelming enough to cause the buyer to cancel the deal, but it is strong enough to create doubt, amplify unresolved objections and even stall implementation. There is an emotional chill following the euphoria of making a purchase decision. What goes up, must come down. So we can give the purchaser a *soft place to land* by using words that comfort them. It is as simple as stating, "You have made an excellent decision," or "We can't wait for you to start enjoying the benefits of this decision."

This is not the time to be wordy. Remember, never sell past the close, which means we do not try to convince the purchaser after they have already made their decision. Once a "yes" is achieved, it's time to move to the Next Steps Phase that represents the tasks involved in finishing the transaction, such as preparing the contract documents or arranging for the delivery of the products. This Next Steps conversation is sprinkled with a few, light affirmation statements.

Acting on the Response

If you receive a yes, please be prepared to know exactly what the next steps are and then engage the post-close process immediately. This needs to be the smoothest part of the entire process. We will have planned, discussed and rehearsed this part with our team so that the Next Steps Phase is seamless and confident. If done properly, the purchaser will feel complete reassurance in your professional guidance through the transition from being just a prospect to becoming a satisfied customer.

Let Silence Be Your Friend

The average salesperson typically does not like silence because it invites an objection, a "no" or "not interested" response from their prospect. Yet, at the close, silence is our best friend. Too often we ask a closing question, have a moment of 'crickets' and then jump in with more features or an unsolicited Alternative Close. This tends to confuse the prospect and causes them to pull back or offer a 'frustration' objection. The close is a time for the strong, calm leader to take over. Using positive confidence, crisp phrases and silence to control the outcome will put us into that leadership position.

Objections at the Close

An objection at close is usually the real objection. This is the one that we absolutely must handle effectively. Learn these words, "besides your concern about the price of our service, is there anything else standing in the way of us moving forward?" If we receive a put-off objection at this point, it is probably because we did not spend enough time identifying needs and closed too early. A put-off objection usually sounds like, "I have to speak with my business partner," or, "I'm just not interested." A response to a put-off at this point might require a reset with Stating the Benefits or Options closes or just a return to needs discovery. This permits more dialogue and questioning to ensure clarity and offers an opportunity to unearth more data points around needs and payoffs.

Don't be afraid to jump back into a productive consultative questioning session so that you are better able to summarize their true needs. It's seems awkward at this point, but it will be worth it, assuming that you have built a strong enough bond and a level of trust that will promote a transparent exchange.

Resistance

Resistance at close comes from an uncovered objection or a lack of urgency. Remember, the best time to handle an objection is before it comes up. So, this usually happens if we did not spend enough time in the questioning phase of the sales conversation to uncover them. If we are getting resistance, it could be an indication that the relationship needs to be improved. A true, trust-based relationship features transparency and openness. Resistance to a Direct Closing question without a detailed objection shows the lack of a transparent conversation. We should seek transparency within the objection or use the Summarize the Benefits Close to position ourselves better.

When is it time to walk away?

Rarely, in our many years of selling and training have we witnessed an emphatic "No". The "No" will come in many forms and our response will be determined by its context or framing. They are usually based on a disguised or latent objection. The danger here is to press too hard with one type of close. This could lead to damage to the relationship in such a way as to make any future effort to move the sale forward non-retrievable.

Deep-sea fishermen know that when the fish strikes the line, they let it run a bit. And don't constantly keep the line tight while reeling the fish in because the line may break or the fish may negotiate its freedom through cunning maneuvers. The technique to reel in a fish is to take our time, be patient, pull some, reel some, wait some, and give some slack or move the boat if we need to. Let's apply the analogy here because the technique to work with a customer under these circumstances is very similar. Given all of the closing options we have discussed, a "no" customer response is an invitation to reconnect with the customer. Simply follow up with questions and then use a different closing technique, thus giving the prospect slack in the line. This takes a conversation immediately out of the closing phase and keeps the environment relaxed and safe to facilitate a good Next Steps conversation.

A partial "yes".

"You know, this sounds good, but...," is a common construction cone in the sales process highway, and we are generally spring-loaded to handle the objection that follows. Do not ignore the beginning of their statement when they say, "This sounds good." Our tactic here should be to explore what sounds good about it. Often, if we do enough work on the area they like, we will jointly find merit in the idea and overcome their objection. Let's use our judgment here and gauge the strength of the relationship we have developed. The Objections Close is best used with this type of buying signal.

Run Silent, Run Deep

We have known buyers who say, "I'll get back to you," and don't. This can be very frustrating. We think, why doesn't the buyer just man-up or woman-up and come back with a "yes", "no", "not ready" or simply state an objection? We have a few choices here and they are dependent upon our relationship with the buyer. We can either wait them out, while remaining in touch, or we can force the issue. We are not recommending one over the other, but if we have people in our own organization that have to make sizeable plans to support the sale, we may need to force the issue using the discussion of this activity as the lever. If we have alternatives to this deal and can sell our goods elsewhere, then we can patiently wait it out. If our pipeline is clogged with buyers that can't make a decision, then we might want to review how we have engaged them in the sales process. Our engagement may be causing their lack of transparency and trust could be the culprit.

TIPS FOR CLOSING

- Know your buyer to determine the best method to use
- Use combination closes to maximize the opportunity
- Stay positive throughout the closing process
- Use silence to give the buyer space to say yes

The Ultimate Close (just for fun)

If we were asking someone to marry us, we would strongly recommend the Direct Method. Just ask and wait for the response. Then, celebrate the "Yes", and take the "No" for what it is. The Indirect Method might be good for testing the waters but once we have gone down that path and we have received little to no resistance, be prepared to ask directly… and soon. Some methods that we would absolutely avoid would be the Opportunity and Summarize the Benefits closing methods. They are overkill and might scare our future life partner into a state of reclusion. And whatever we do, do not use the Weighing Method. While creating a list of plusses and minuses might be therapeutic for the relationship, it is a train wreck way of popping the question. Try that one after your 1st anniversary and then seek professional help if necessary.

Summary for Closing the Gap

In this section, we have given you a multitude of closing methods and combinations. Take this knowledge and do all you can to make closing conversations as natural as possible. It only takes confidence and a positive attitude built on the foundation of the successful, consistent application of the entire sales process. Just remember, the closing dialogue will only be as successful as our ability to summarize our customer's needs. The quest to identify that need is what drives the sales process engine. Once that need is satisfied and the gap is closed, we can celebrate this success with our new customer!

CHAPTER 4

Embrace the Prospecting Process

An excellent sales process is a roadmap to successful selling. However, there is one key ingredient that comes before the formal sales process. This is the ability to generate and convert qualified leads into mature, legitimate opportunities. Fortunately, there is a process that we will reveal in this section, around which we can plan our activities to place qualified leads in our pipeline with a strong expectation of closing the sale.

With a lead in hand, the timing to close is defined by the sales cycle. A computer sale might take 30 minutes; a home sale could be take 3 months and a large piece of capital equipment possibly 2 years. This is the sales cycle to which we plan our activities in order to close the sale. When prospecting, developing skills in "hunting"—prospecting for new opportunities and "farming"—looking for opportunities in existing accounts, is essential. Using that metaphor, we are best positioned to hunt and farm when we are in 'prospect rich' territory with the right skills, process and tools in hand.

The Prospecting Process provides structure to prepare the mindset and muscle required in the initial phase of any sales process. We intend to provide the motivation, inspiration, skills, tools and best practices to be successful during this process. Bear in mind that the 12 Principles of Selling are ever-present throughout the prospecting process, so we should find opportunities to exhibit and engage them as we implement this process.

Let's get started. Prospecting requires an even stronger 'inner game' than the sales process because we are usually standing consistently at the edge of our comfort zone. Prospecting requires us to venture towards new industries or territories in, which we might be unfamiliar. It will absolutely require us to meet new people and deal with the full palate of personality styles while we intentionally expand our business network of contacts. The inspiration and motivation needed for us to make this a daily effort challenges the depths of our inner strength. Selling, especially prospecting, is not for the shy wallflower but does not require a bold and boastful persona. We just need to be strong, calm, organized and persistent. Prospecting challenges our mental toughness unlike any other part of the sales process. We need a balance of thinking and doing at a high level. It's time to embrace the challenge and make prospecting the most invigorating part of our activities. Lean into it, look forward to it and make it the adventure in our professional life.

As sales professionals, we understand the important role prospecting plays in the sales results. We were often asked for a realistic assessment of our sales goals, as a basis for our incentive plan. Management always increased our goals by 20%, which was actually in our best interest because it made us aim for a higher goal. Or, like a business we recently worked with, their salespeople were no longer incentivized by sustaining their current book of business, but rather by the amount of new clients they brought into the customer mix. Now, the focus was solely on prospecting. So, let's take a look at a strategic approach to our prospecting campaign.

Prospecting Process

We have divided the prospecting process into two distinct phases, Strategy and Execution. Strategy is planning and organizing for the prospecting activity and execution is the follow though of the actionable plans created during the Strategy phase.

Step 1: Strategy – the planning phase

- Vision – Keeping the end in mind to inspire and motivate yourself.
- Goals – Making sure you are conducting the right activities.
- Resources – Finding your prospects and putting qualified leads in the pipeline.

Step 2: Execution – the action phase

- Contact Plan – Preparing yourself for that first contact.
- Contact Action – Managing the first contact.
- Cultivate leads – Managing the lead after the first contact.

Strategy

We are conducting strategic planning all of the time in our personal and professional lives. We just may not realize we are doing it. Any good strategic plan starts with a vision of what we want to achieve. It is a mind picture of what the successful end result might look like. In our case, it could be a sales goal or targeting new opportunities within an existing account. Our goal might be 20 private home sales closes this year. Or it could be to position our data cloud management system for a sure win for the upcoming industry request for this fall. Whether our vision/goal was given to us or is something that we established ourselves, we must make it the centerpiece in our mind game. It becomes a motivational tool and drives the daily execution of our action plan. Without our vision/goal in focus, we will find inconsistencies in our execution. What we do daily will eventually become comfortable, and therefore cause us to plateau, so we must consistently challenge ourselves to push past our comfort zones and engage in increasingly more challenging activities.

For the strategy segment of our prospecting journey, we should first plan our activity goals. Next, we will refine our lead generation engine and then gather the resources necessary to begin executing our plan. Our prospecting plan requires that we ensure all activities are the "right" activities to maximize our close rate. A good way to accomplish this is to examine the effectiveness of our activities, then create actionable tasks driven by smaller goals, which will contribute to our close rate.

Plan Your Prospecting Activities

Before we set out to make face-to-face, email or telephone-prospecting calls there is much work to do. We first need to get smart about who we need to contact and how we will go about doing it. There was a day when prospecting meant plowing through the yellow pages or parking at an office park and walking from business to business to play "gatekeeper croquet". It's just not done that way so much anymore. Now we need to be on the inside of the Internet chat room for your target industry, be a part of a group of industry insiders, be the rock star at the networking event or plugged into a referral wheelhouse.

Buyers are changing, and more often than in the past, they are seeking a 'low effort' approach. By this, we mean that they want to 'press a button' and have high quality products and services delivered to their doorstep, with instant payment options and robust support tools at the lowest possible cost. Relationships, while very important, often must be supported by benign, impersonal service and support tools that can solve problems and answer questions on the spot. This provides an opportunity to partner with our marketing professionals, whose role it is to create products that effectively position and support our company, products and services. Also, many of these products should be positioned in the virtual marketplace, where many buyers are turning to make their buying decisions. We should not use inadequate marketing resources as an excuse for our lack of initiative. It is always up to the sales professional to fill the gaps with a strong personal reputation, effective customer engagement and a strong lead generation plan.

New, youthful buyers in the marketplace don't have lengthy industry relationships and are going to Google, Bing or Yahoo searches to find qualified vendors with products and services that meet their needs, at a good value. Marketing needs to find a way to get the name of our company on "page one" of the Google search engine, because that is the prime real estate that is driving many business decisions today. If at all possible, they also need a plan to dominate the web space for our brand name and product category, in addition to the search terms related to our products/services. This approach will be even more important as the Internet experience continues to mature in the future. For example, just witness the availability of real estate and automobile purchase tools that basically provide elaborate specifications, previous owner history, performance ratings and price comparison tools. This is the world to which buyers, and the general public, are becoming more accustomed. Therefore, as salespeople we need to understand this world and work with our companies to innovate systems that will help differentiate ourselves from the competition.

It is understandable that we may not be able to dominate the web space for our products or services. Creating web search engine energy takes time and intentional effort, but we do need to have an online presence that positively reflects our "professional brand" when a prospect conducts an Internet search for us. Every time someone clicks on our link(s), it creates search engine relevance that will eventually help your online presence and search positioning. For planning purposes, our online and offline activities should enhance our reputation in all respects. Let's revisit the importance of an essential offline activity, networking, as a means of lead generation. Using a networking event to just make lead contacts does not address the whole picture for a professional salesperson. Networking events are truly about building relationships and helping you to become known as a valuable resource. Who we know is important but who knows us is critical to networking success. Refer to Principle 7 for more information about the true purpose of networking.

Industry trade shows are also effective for the more complex or technical sale. Whether we are walking a show or working from a booth, our mission goes beyond just getting business cards, collecting giveaways and finding leads. Our activities should also include attending industry presentations and gathering customer and competitive marketing materials to increase our marketplace knowledge. We should always go to these events with a plan of action and an agenda. Most industry trade shows have apps that exhibit a calendar of events and the booth location of paying participants. If one exists, download it, plan from it and use it during the show. To repeat, it's not who you know, it's who knows you that adds to our value in the market.

This is meant to drive home the point that we do our best work when we have a positive reputation to maintain in the industry and these efforts will be a constant work in progress. We should continue to build our personal charisma, share our industry and product group with other stakeholders and join industry groups with the intent of eventually assuming a leadership role within the group. Remember, in industry networking events, the one person in the room that everyone seems to know, usually is the organizer and we should promote ourselves to this role as soon as we are able. Networking events will always work well for most product types because they allow us to establish relationships within a "less than formal" environment and at some point these relationships can develop in customers or referral sources. We've established that it is important to be known, be found, be respected and be credible. Prospecting for new business is more complex than generating business from clients that already love us and our products. This requires more forethought toward intentional acts. So just what do we need to plan before we burn some shoe leather?

Set Goals and Measure Your Prospecting Activities

Goal setting involves breaking down the activities of prospecting into one of these three areas; either they are a contribution, a conversion or a close. Goals, as defined for the prospecting process, are the set of actions that will be taken to achieve a desired number of closed deals. For example, we set a goal of 5 closed deals for the quarter, month or year. We have analyzed that we have achieved 5 closed deals in the past by contacting 100 qualified leads. Our activities through the pipeline yield a 5% conversion rate. Here are the activities based on this scenario. For instance:

Leads contacted (45 Internet leads, 55 cold)	100
Allowed to establish credibility	30
Allowed to question	21
Allowed to present solution	11
Closes	5
Conversion Rate	5%

For the true conversion rate, we want to examine the source of the leads to determine which leads were generating the better result, such as, warm leads provided by marketing, referrals, the Internet, or cold calls. Examining the type of lead will help us determine our most successful lead generation technique. We then take the opportunity to move leads, that don't convert, to a touch point tool allowing us to remain in contact via email at regular intervals.

Once we have identified our prospecting activities, measured goals designed to improve our conversion rate can be set. We have the following 3 choices to improve conversion rate:

- Increase the quantity of your leads.
- Increase the quality of your leads.
- Improve the quality of your interactions with your leads.

To increase the quantity of leads let's examine how we can improve our lead generation techniques.

It's time to take inventory of the way we are securing leads now and what might be available to us going forward. There are companies out there that provide, what they call, 'warm' lead lists. They charge on a per lead basis and this avenue saves time, energy and the challenges associated with mining our own leads. The downside of these services is that the contact information may not be accurate or current. If we are fortunate enough to have an internal resource that can validate the information, and even generate an appointment through lead contacting, we are living in luxury. Otherwise, expect to spend some time distilling the information provided. Don't let this become frustrating, just remember, we have to move a lot of dirt to find gold. Take every opportunity on our own, or with our peers, to brainstorm new methods of lead generation.

Becoming better at qualifying our prospects is the best way to speed up our conversion time and increase our conversion rate. We qualify our prospects in the following ways:

Probability to buy – Are they ready to buy now? Is the solution we offer a right fit for their needs and does it meet their specifications or certification?

<u>Timing to buy</u> – Are they buying now or is there a budget cycle that drives their purchasing activity.

<u>Size of opportunity</u> – Is the return from the opportunity worth the time, energy and resources needed to secure the business?

<u>Probability of switching</u> – Is the competition entrenched to a point where the cost of the prospect to switch is prohibitive?

These factors are important and their contribution to the overall decision to qualify the prospect with a high or low ranking can be weighted to create a true priority list. We examine it this way to ensure that we are working on the right opportunities first. We tend to work on opportunities that help us maintain our position in our comfort zone. Using a process of prioritizing opportunities is a good practice. Time is a non-renewable resource and working on non-productive opportunities can be the biggest time thief we may face

Improve Follow up Touch Point Generation Tools

We mentioned that timing is key to successful prospecting. So, if the prospect is not quite ready today, for whatever reason, it is important to keep in contact with them on a regular basis. Most CRM (customer relationship management) systems have these tools to facilitate this activity and we should not consider using one that does not. If we do not have a CRM tool to utilize, we should at least put a basic reminder "tickler" system in place. For example, many reps use the calendar function on their phone or laptop simply to remind them when it's time to reach back out to their prospect. We must make sure that we also set contact intervals that make sense to our prospects, especially if they have fixed RFPs, contract renewals or budget development schedules that would drive their buying activities. Either way, it is best to automate this process if at all possible; it will save us time to pursue more leads.

Execution

So we have developed a list of qualified leads, prioritized them and are now prepared to make contact. It's time to put mind and muscle to work. The mind piece is planning the conversation. This involves some scripting and rehearsing. Please refer back to the elements of the sales process as they apply here in the areas of conducting successful sales conversations. Also, the 12 Principles are ever present in all of our sales activities.

Contact Plan

Who will we be speaking with? Remember it all starts with the prospect's name, so let us be diligent about using their name. After all, people love the sound of their own name. Beyond that, we use LinkedIn, the Google search function or referral sources to learn about our prospect and remember the first step in our sales process, "Build a Bond". This is the best way to make an instant connection. If we are speaking to someone who was referred to us, we want to mention our referral source immediately as a way to establishing common ground. Most buyers find comfort in doing business with people with whom they share something in common.

We should know our objective. If the purpose of the call is to set an appointment, then set that expectation early in the conversation. Knowing how we are going to open the call or start the conversation will be essential to getting off on the right foot. Having the first sentence or two prepared will give us confidence to launch into a customer-focused conversation. We generally open with the purpose of the call and a benefit to the prospect. Then, we have our credentials statement prepared and ready to deliver it, whether we are leaving a voicemail or actually speaking with our prospect. The voicemail credentials statement can be somewhat scripted but don't make it sound that way. In our workshops, we actually have the participants record their statement to their own voicemail to listen to it for self-coaching purposes. Feel free to visit www.salesuniverse.com for more details.

Improve the Quality of Your Conversations during the Prospecting Process

Knowing our conversion rate based on prospecting activities is key to setting the right goals. Usually the conversion rate is a simple ratio between the number of leads contacted, the number presentations delivered, and the number of closes. The obvious suggestion to increase the number of closes would simply be to increase the number of leads contacted, but there is a more effective method of increasing our conversion rate. What if we did not increase the number of leads contacted, but improved the quality of the communications with those leads? By simply improving the quality of our conversations, we will increase the number of presentations and produce a higher rate of closes with the same lead count. Participants in our workshops have returned to tell us that their ability to deliver more effective openings, supported by valued driven credentials statements, combined with an effective and efficient questioning strategy, has resulted in higher conversion rates.

Many in the sales training field often mutter, "…It's just a numbers game." Don't believe this statement completely, because even though we need the numbers up front, if we fail to provide quality treatment of these opportunities with our prospects, then we are mismanaging the numbers. The buyer became our "lead" because eventually, they are going to purchase the products we sell – either from our competitor or us. Keeping the lead in play means valuing every phase of our communication with them.

Voice mail (keep it brief)

Announce your name, company and a brief credentials statement. Always leave our phone number twice, once at the beginning and once at the end. This is so they have a chance to write it down. Speak slowly with excellent diction. If this is a second or third call, leave a 'sticky note' instead of a credentials statement. A sticky note is a compelling feature or fact of your product/service with a linking benefit that will surely resonate with your prospect. It should be based on an assumed, general need that hits the mark for the sticky note to be effective. Keep the message long enough to be meaningful, interesting and inviting yet concise enough not to annoy — 20 – 30 seconds should do it.

Actual Contact with the Lead

Should we be fortunate enough to make a successful contact, our goal is to keep them on the phone long enough to achieve our primary objective. The conversation flow is:

Name + company + Who referred us (if applicable) + Purpose + Credentials + statement + Question + Objective + Recommend Action.

If the objective is to make an appointment, then we need to be prepared with a short, persuasive credentials statement to generate interest, check-in, listen for affirmative buying signals and ask for the appointment. If your goal is a 'First Call, Only Call' and you need to close during that interchange, then the next section is for you.

First Call, Only Call

We have trained and coached many telesales groups for both outbound and inbound prospects. Their goal, once they have made contact with a decision maker, is to introduce the opportunity, discover needs, position their solution and then close the sale. In many cases, they do all this in less than 10 minutes Always remember, our customers have limited time and possible alternatives to our solution, so we need to be on top of our game in this world.

The success of a 'First Call, Only Call' exchange is using the sales process at an accelerated pace. We recommend developing a conversation flow template that will work specifically for your business and a typical call scenario. Then use the template to rehearse and role-play. Be sure to throw in some objections that will certainly come up in order to make it as realistic as possible.

Gatekeepers

We generally refer to "gatekeepers" as the Vice President of first impressions because their initial impression of us will carry a lot of weight with our prospect. No, there is no school for professional gatekeepers. They are good at what they do because of their passion to execute on their charge, to protect the decision makers' time, energy and calendar. We need to build rapport and a relationship with them. After all, we are building relationships with everyone we meet that are involved in any way with the success of our sales effort. Be charming and always professional.

Just as the subject line on an email is a gateway to exposure, the credentials statement for a gatekeeper is just as important. Remember their charge, so our credentials statement has to be compelling in such a way that the gatekeeper can perceive value enough to pass that message along. Gatekeepers can fall into a few categories that require a unique approach for each:

The Front Desk—The best approach is to take in the surroundings and assess what is viewed as important to the business. Having first and last names and a fall back contact is always helpful. The more we are able to suggest that we are expected, the better our chances of making progress. In the absence of effective pre-approach information, be naturally curious and use the gatekeeper as a means to educate ourselves on what is important to our prospect. Ask about the best way to make an appointment or who to speak with in lieu of this individual.

The Administrative Assistant

Voicemail – Being brief is best. This should be something that is scripted unless we are very confident in our ability to be clear, concise and to the point. Just remember, if we are not happy with our message, we may not have another opportunity to correct it, so let us make it count.

Direct contact – If we have the pleasure of speaking with the administrative assistant, keep the following process in mind:

Name...Company...Who referred us (if applicable)... Purpose...Credentials statement...Leave message

Prospecting Process Assessment

Let's take time to assess the success of our prospecting activities, in an ever-increasing effort to improve our close rate. As we have mentioned, our close rate improves through the quality of prospects entering our pipeline in addition to the quality of the conversations we have with them. This is an activity that will ensure our efficiency as a prospector. Let's ask ourselves the following questions.

1. Where did the lead come from and then how far did they move through the process?

   Assessing this area will determine the source of our most productive leads.
2. Where does the movement of the prospect through our pipeline stop?

   An examination here represents an opportunity to improve our skills in that area. If, for instance, we are making presentations of our solutions to prospects but not moving them to close, we may need to improve the following: our ability to assess client need, our ability to present the value of our solutions or our ability to assess if something has changed with the prospect which has stalled our progress.

3. How long is the typical contact-to-close (velocity through our pipeline)?

   Examine this by lead category. This will determine the prospecting sales cycle based on lead type. If we have found that leads generated through online tools have the quickest contact-to-close cycle, then we should bolster our tools to strengthen that category.
4. What are our prospecting Strengths, Weakness, Opportunities, and Threats (SWOT)? Create a four-quadrant matrix for each of these considerations and conduct an assessment of your prospecting approach. This is an honest personal assessment of your ability to prospect and a great exercise to reveal the effectiveness of your prospecting strategy and execution. Perform a SWOT analysis with a peer in your sales group if at all possible and compare notes to make this exercise most effective.
5. How often do we conduct a conversion rate brainstorm session? With a peer-partner, we should conduct a brainstorming session that examines any possible activities or improvements that can increase our conversion rate. Remember, we want to be operating at the highest possible success level, with the least possible effort. This will be time well spent with that goal in mind.

TIPS FOR EFFECTIVE PROSPECTING

- Measure your activities' effectiveness
- Perform results-producing activities (for example – activities that produce qualified leads for follow up later.

- Focus on improving the quality of the prospecting conversation
- Continue to provide value to your prospects, even when they don't buy right away

Summary for Embracing the Prospecting Process

Before the sales process starts, the pipeline must be filled with qualified prospects. The activities that lead up to and encompass the prospecting process are critical to ensure the highest possible close rate and the happiest customers. We know that timing is paramount to having a successful strategic prospecting campaign. Customers don't usually buy unless they have a need for our product/service and see an advantage to buying now. So a 100% success rate is reserved for those who are very good, very lucky or are a sole source provider for their category of business. A hearty action plan that includes both an effective prospecting strategy and consistent execution is a must to position us well for success in this area.

CHAPTER 5

Master Your Negotiations

A negotiation is a place where customers and business people iron out differences and construct agreements. Negotiation conversations and sales conversation share some similarities and differences. In a sales conversation, we are seeking transparency and openness while developing a positive relationship along with closing the deal. The negotiation conversation has some of these elements, with some significant differences. In this conversation, both parties seek to gain a successful outcome seeking favorable terms, usually in the area of price and specifications. This sets up a game table.

Remember that selling is the first step to a successful deal and negotiation is the second. We often begin the negotiation process too soon by offering concessions early, like moving price points or important terms, during the selling phase. We may do this in the interest of building a stronger relationship but often it results in our inability to bargain later. Likewise, we may say or do something in the negotiation process that jeopardizes the relationship. So striking a balance between the sales process, the negotiation process and the efforts to strengthen our relationships is critical.

Beginning the negotiation early may work well for a less complex sale such as the 'First Call, Only Call' or a retail sale. In these situations, the customer walks in with a need and walks out with our product but in a more complex sale, this is best left for the negotiation table, where concessions are traded not donated. When we sell we are building value, which strengthens our position to defend our value when the client tries to negotiate it away. Both sides should participate in the world of give and take. So the best arena for that discussion is after the client is sold and they now want to discuss bringing our solution in. The negotiation conversation can quickly evolve from checkers, to chess, to poker. We become more careful with our words and each party is more closely reading intent though body language, voice inflection and other 'tells'. Some negotiators even resort to outbursts or benign responses to evoke an emotional response or to throw the other party "off their game". All of the sudden we see 'stakes in the ground' and threats to walk away from the deal which are common, acceptable tactics to establish the parameters of the discussion. A sales conversation ends when the prospect says "yes" and means it. The negotiation ends when the salesperson says "no." Becoming a master at negotiation is a must and it involves a process to ensure the creation of a positive plan, the faithful execution of that plan and the eventual achievement of our desired outcome.

Like the sales process, the one who is most prepared has the advantage in the negotiation process. Effective negotiations require an examination of the best possible outcome and a visualization of the steps to get there. We have the power to envision the entire negotiation in our mind which will help us to predict the maneuvers that will be required to reach our goal. So, let's take advantage of that ability and use it to prepare ourselves by examining the negotiation process and its essential elements.

The stages of the negotiation process:

- Setting the game table
- Planning our strategy and tactics
- Maneuvering
- Use leverage
- "All in"—The end game
- Wrapping the package

Setting the Table

Our first act is to get organized, to pull all of the information related to the negotiation together and put all of the cards on the table in front of us. These cards include but are certainly not limited to the following:

- Cost vs. price analysis (includes target margin)
- Sources of value (such as after-sale support, installation and scalability)
- General terms (such as payment, delivery, insurance, warranty and liability)

Use a method of weighing the importance of each element so we can determine which element we would be willing to yield at the table or fight to maintain. We also want to assess which elements are more important to our customer for the same reasons. We suggest the creation of a negotiation (spreadsheet) tool that lists all of the elements so they can be easily referenced during the negotiation process. Also, have some alternate scenarios already planned out, for example, if we have room for price reduction in exchange for a value exchange, then let's have a spreadsheet with the outline of the range of our price vs. the analysis of the cost. It is also important that we have all necessary executive approvals for the moves we may make during the negotiation process.

Of high importance in our planning process is to be aware of who will be seated on the other side of the table. We also want to know if there will be influence wielded by persons not in attendance during our negotiation process. Know the names and roles of the individuals, their level of influence and stake in a negotiated settlement. We do this to isolate what would be important to them and to know who to persuade as we conduct our session(s). Also, if we have any prior experience or knowledge with this customer to draw upon, we should list their past behaviors and negotiation style, then strategize against it.

Planning Our Strategy and Tactical Moves

We negotiate to both advance and preserve our interests. The same is true for those sitting across the table from us. Our interests are the high ground that looms over our discussions. When the customer bought our product or service, they were responding to a heightened need that had to be satisfied. It is important to re-emphasize that need throughout the negotiation process. The need was likely related to reducing cost, or improving quality or creating efficiencies. This remains the anchor for our negotiation discussions. Create a statement that summarized their main interest(s) for this negotiation to be successful and keep it as a central part of the planning phase. This will restrain us from arguing over minutia later on. If the decision to buy has not yet been made, we must still maintain the prospect's primary interest as central to the discussion. Their ability to attain their desired outcome, by the utilization of our product/services, must be apparent at all times.

I (Charles) once led a business team in a negotiation to supply original equipment components with a major corporate business jet manufacturer. As part of the new rules of engagement for OEM's in the aviation business, the contract negotiation is conducted and finished before the award is made to the prospective supplier(s). Procurement departments now understand that they have more leverage in negotiation if conducted before the award rather than after. They can use competition to obtain more favorable terms. We learned during the negotiation that they had no budget for our components for the new construction aircraft and had to make up for that by selling the parts as a distributor from the two suppliers selected to the aftermarket. So they were trying to get the best aftermarket discount they could. Once we realized that they had no budget and that was the main driver for their interests, we completely changed the game. We offered the components for the new production aircraft at no cost. In exchange we offered to be the only, sole source, supplier for this component. Their overall savings was in the millions of dollars for the new production aircraft budget and they still have the opportunity to distribute the part in the aftermarket. This was unorthodox for them to have a sole source supplier for this component, but it satisfied their interest so they agreed and chased our competitor away. Discover and negotiate around the client interests to find the best results.

With the elements organized, we can now set about the task of planning our conversations and moves at the table. There are several important considerations that must be addressed in the planning phase before any dialogue begins. These terms are defined below so we can determine when to tactically discuss or use them as part of our negotiation strategy.

Walk Away

Most complex negotiations become more intense when both parties have reached the edge of their negotiation parameters. These areas are usually related to cost, time and quality. The customer will likely have a target price and an absolute bottom line acceptable price. How will we know? They will stay at the table for their target price but will threaten to walk away for their bottom line price. If they were trained by one of our negotiation consultants, they will continue to ask for what they want until they are certain that they cannot get more. A walk away is the strongest observable buying signal. Watch for it and know how you will counter. Use it to protect your interests.

Position

We take up a *position* around what we consider to be the essential elements of the deal. These are the thesis of the discussion that you and the client conduct during the negotiation. They are the features of the contract and are central to the agreement. These features are usually described as price, payment, delivery, performance, warranty, and liability and specification compliance.

Interests

Our *interest* can be defined as the motivation behind positions. We work to advance and protect our interest. Interests are broad and are usually associated with cost, time and quality. When the client's interests are understood, then their positions are more coherent. There is a difference between a need and an interest. A bank customer needs a lower interest rate, but has an interest in preserving their cash from month to month. Arguing over the rate is a no win game. Discussing how the client can preserve cash is catering to their interest.

Parameters

Parameter is defined as the boundary of the parties' position in the negotiation. They are the limits we have set on the flexibility of positions around critical features of the deal. If they cannot accept the deal above a certain price then we have reached the limit of their price position. Any movement of price that doesn't violate the limit during the discussion is within the *parameters* of the price feature of the deal.

Take note when we are bumping up against their parameters with respect to certain positions. They will reveal their limits through their behaviors. This does not necessarily mean that we have reached an insurmountable limit, but might mean that we will have to bargain or 'chip' away at the position by trading other interests to craft a deal. For instance, the client might have a price ceiling above which they would not agree, but could move the price position beyond their limit if they could take advantage of more favorable payment or interest terms.

Leverage

Leverage can be simply defined as the strength of your position during the negotiation. And, this is determined by the magnitude of need either you or your client have for a successful outcome. Whoever needs this transaction to be concluded more urgently or sooner than the other party, may end up yielding some leverage. For example, if we need to make this sale to reach our quota, we may be inclined to "blink" first at the negotiation table. Similarly, if the client needs our solution now to meet an operational deadline, then they may "blink" first and we therefore have the leverage.

Knowing when we have leverage and when we don't is essential for creating the right strategy for these discussions. During our questioning phase, while we are ascertaining their needs, we would also be well advised to seek information about how soon and how desperately they need a (different) solution. We do this to determine the amount of leverage we might have should we be fortunate enough to negotiate a deal together. If our prospect has a sense of urgency, we will likely have the leverage and we should plan our strategy accordingly. For example, we could increase their sense of urgency by strategically slowing the negotiations down as part of our strategy. This may increase their anxiety and improve our position. Also, we can frame the benefits and payoffs of our products, in relation to our clients' needs, in a manner to create urgency by reminding them of the consequences of not taking action. Another way is to help your client to create a picture in their mind of them enjoying the benefits of your solution. In all cases, the better we are at creating a sense of urgency, the greater our ability to create leverage.

Non-negotiable Terms

No doubt there will be some seemingly immovable items that have been or will be identified during the discussions. Make some assumptions about what those might be ahead of time. For instance, we may insist upon certain legal terms such as auto-renewal or warranty terms that will be non-negotiable. They may have liquidated damages for performance deficiencies that need to be included in any agreement they sign as a matter of procurement policy. Knowing these non-negotiable terms makes them 'chips' at the table. Using these as leverage for other terms we desire is just the application of good negotiation skills. Leave your emotions out of their unwillingness to modify language and use it to your advantage.

Sources of Value

Every product or service has cost components that serve as the basis for price. We need to understand what these components are during the negotiation and be able to explain, at a top level, their contribution. They include the cost of materials, labor, research and development, testing, marketing, plant equipment, services related to quality assurance and reliability, warehousing, distribution, etc. The value of these elements to the client are what we call *sources of value*. We should know the financial contribution each of these components adds to the price. And, we should know which of these components are most important to the client.

Sources of value are those things that are also deliverables with the product or service. They might be the support services, warranty, and performance of the product vs. the competition, payment terms and options, delivery terms and conditions, or packaging. All of these value sources are worth something. When negotiating price points, it is wise to exchange them for sources of value. Say, "I can give a percentage on price, but I will have to give up this other source of value over here. For this one percent we will have to reconsider early payment discount or extended payment terms." Exchanges at the table like these are important. So we must always be aware of the sources of value for the buyer. Here are some additional sources of value: Free install, training, upgrades, trial periods, early installation, free setup, fixed prices for future purchases, extended warranties, payment terms, performance guarantees. This list should be expanded during a peer brainstorming session to ensure we have all possible sources for our industries. Once we are aware of all possible sources of value, and know which of these are meaningful to our customer, we will be able to use them as bargaining chips to exchange at the table to entice commitment. Most often they should be used in lieu of dropping our price.

Best Alternative to a Negotiated Agreement (BATNA)

Another source of leverage is to have an alternative outlet for the products we trying to sell. When we have an alternative to the deal that allows us to move our products or capacity to make our products to another buying source at an equivalent or greater return, we call this a *BATNA*. If we have another customer that also wants our products and our capacity to produce additional products is limited, then we are in the unique position to sell to the highest bidder. Also, if we have a large quantity of opportunities in our pipeline, we can go after other business in lieu of the current deal. Having a strong BATNA gives us leverage in the negotiation because it reduces our need to reach this specific deal.

Thus we can establish narrower parameters around which to negotiation our positions.

Here is a perfect Example of Leverage based upon BATNA. Harley Davidson has, for years, been able to sell their motorcycles at full list price without the need to discounting to close deals because of the huge demand for their products. Given that their capacity to produce enough product to meet the demand is limited (perhaps by design), they can always sell all of the motorcycles they produce to willing, enthusiastic buyers.

Their customers want the product with urgency which gives Harley Davidson a strong position. The brand image they have created and promoted through quality performance and excellent service represent true sources of value and strengthen their price and term positions.

Maneuvering

An interesting feature of negotiations is the chance for either party to grab control of the discussion. Some believe that the one who controls the agenda, discussion and the moves at the table will have an advantage. We are less inclined to universally adopt that philosophy. Maneuvering is just executing our plan and reacting to situations with fact-based responses and proposals. Let's review some maneuvers.

Who Opens? It Depends

There are two schools of thought regarding who should open the discussion. Some experts advise that we should open when we are in a position of strength and have sufficient leverage. That suggests that if we are in a weaker position, we yield opening to the other party and react. Since the opening serves the purpose of positioning our offer, there is no downside to crafting an effective opening and using it. A universal rule is to always be prepared to open. If for some reason the buyer chose to do so or just takes the reigns, then we can respond appropriately. Having our opening prepared does provide some mental confidence that will carry through the negotiation.

Maneuvering Around Price

In our negotiation skills workshops, the elephant in the room is the discussion around price. The participants are usually hungry for knowledge about why buyers always want to make the conversations about price. And of course, they want to know how they should respond. Buyers want to make our product or service a commodity. For them, this makes price the most significant issue to discuss. They will tell us that what we are offering is not different in quality and value than any competitive brand. Thus making our solution just a commodity. Should they successful position us in this way, they can focus on reducing price to real their successful outcome.

Lets' assume that we did not drop our price during the sales conversation. We should have preserved some room for price maneuvering and now, by taking control of this part of the discussion, we can learn how to best position ourselves to preserve our price points. This is our opportunity to examine the success we can have by using our non-price sources of value, during the discussion. Our trainers teach buyers to constantly ask for a lower price and they will keep asking, until they are assured by the salesperson's words and tone, that they are getting the best value possible. Only then will they be motivated to stop asking for a lower price.

We should always avoid unilaterally lowering your price. The act of unilaterally dropping price points compromises trust. To give up empty price points tells the buyer that we weren't honest with our price offering from the very start. That dishonesty just takes leverage away from us and there is no assurance that this will stop them from continuously asking for a better deal. When the buyer sees 'lower price' blood in the water, the feeding frenzy to pursue an even lower price will continue.

As Benjamin Franklin said, *"He gives twice that gives soon, and will be soon asked to give again."*[17]

We should choose to discuss price when it is our time to do so. Note that our buyer may nominate the 'price' topic early and often because they want to make our product more of a commodity, in an effort to gain leverage. They desire a lower price and they will continue to ask for it. So when they say, "…lets address your high price." Simply respond by saying, "…I see that you want to make sure you're getting the best value. Let me assure you that you are. We can discuss that further after we address the value that makes our price so attractive." Defer the price discussion to a point in the negotiations when it serves our interests. As we have mentioned before, price points are not to be exchanged unilaterally. We fight for every fraction of a percent by explaining the true value of our price.

If you must discount, always avoid using round numbers. Telling the buyer that we can move 3% appears random. Telling the buyer that we can move 2.78% appears to be studied and tells the buyer that we have calculated value to lowest denominator. This also suggests that any movement in price or terms is done in small increments, and any discounting is a court of last resort.

Move with Options Rather Than Price Points

During our training sessions, we ask the participants to list the options-beyond-price movement they have available to them. These often include for example, payment terms, early delivery, extended warranties, increased volume, etc. as was discussed in the "sources of value" section. We ask for 10 options-beyond-price and then state, "If you could not move price, what could you offer instead." We also ask them to combine options and discuss the benefit to the buyer in doing so. Knowing options and planning their use in response to price pressure is a good tactic.

In our workshops for buyers, we train to always ask for concessions in many forms. Their asking is often disguised by making demands on our time, energy and resources. They may ask for more detailed information or a breakdown of cost structure that is included in the profit margin. They may also make a preposterous offer just to take us off center so they can widen the offer gap making a 'split-the-difference scenario more attractive for their purpose.

For example, during a contract negotiation, where the deal was for multi-million dollar, multi-year agreement, all of the elements of the deal were complete and both teams expressed satisfaction in the final product. Then the agreement was elevated to the mahogany row executives at the buying organization for signature. That's when the real bargaining took place. The senior executive asked for "a final call," and while the prices remained intact, there was a final movement around how the prices were to be escalated over the term of the agreement. We should always be prepared. As the cliché says, "the deal is not done until the ink is dry."

Use Leverage

The one true area of leverage buyers have is their authority to buy from us or to send us packing. They always have one more yes-or-no choice than we do. Beyond that, buyers are trained to create leverage where there may not be any. How do the buyers do this? They do this by creating the appearance of leverage, such as stating that our price is too high or the competition has a better solution, which may not be true at all. These may simply be empty statements to create leverage. Would they truly tell a fib? Yes, and it is all part of maneuvering on the game table. Our job is to discover their interests and keep the conversation centered on how our solution satisfies their interests. By continuing to ask them to clarify their puffed statements, we can discern their validity.

"All In" And the End Game

The end of the negotiation has some similarities to the end of the sales process. Review the closing section of the sales process to find some ideas about how to bring the negotiation to its conclusion. Most likely the end of the negotiation is a combination of a Direct Close with Next Steps.

Wrapping the Package

The final steps of the negotiation process are critically important. Depending on the complexity of the negotiation, we are well advised to set realistic expectations about document handling which includes routing, signatures and actions related to early deliverables. If there is a chance a zealous executive could alter the unsigned document during the routing cycle, say so. If we are part of a large organization and the routing cycle could take some time, say so. Setting the proper expectations here can preserve the good relationship that we have built through the sales and negotiation process.

TIPS FOR EFFECTIVE SALES NEGOTIATORS

- Prepare, Prepare, prepare
- Know your leverage and options
- Talk about price when you are ready
- Have a list of "sources of value" we can exchange instead of making price concessions

Summary for Mastering your Negotiations

Professional sales people are exceptional negotiators and know what to keep and what to trade. Some negotiations are a part of the sales process and must be completed in order to close the sale. For more complex transactions, the negotiation begins when the sale is closed. Knowing the difference is important because we want to make sure we preserve our margin and terms of the deal that are most important to us. Most times, we are also preserving the relationship with the client and the perception our client carries for our brand. Negotiating well is best learned by doing. We have given you the knowledge you need to excel, now use it and win.

A Final Word

Successful, charismatic people who are achieving at a high level create a personal wake. For example, one of the most engaged corporate learning and development leaders, Janet McCormick discusses the concept, that our personal behaviors, attitudes and actions create ripples just like the wake on a boat. A boat's wake affects the objects around it and the faster the boat moves, the more impact the wake will have. If a boat goes too fast, with people nearby, those people will get rocked. Using this analogy, it is vitally important for us to be aware of how our own personal wake affects the people around us. Our ability to make personal connections, demonstrate credibility and build trust will depend on this self-awareness. This is not relegated to just our customer relationships. The people within our own organization who work providing us support in our effort to be successful will feel our wake. Our peers and our management will also be affected. The principles of "everyone counts, let them know" and "develop your personal brand" are central to our ability to be effective as a leader in our space. We do not operate in a vacuum and our ability to deliver the highest quality service to our customers is also dependent upon the relationships we have with stakeholders within our own organization.

Many organizations have departments that the sales teams view as the "sales prevention team." For example, it could be the credit, underwriting or the compliance departments. The relationship between sales and these groups can often be adversarial. We must challenge ourselves to build personal relationships with these types of teams and their leadership. A process for collaborative communications with these departments often will drive better quality sales and result in a stronger book of business for the salesperson.

We, as sales professionals, are constantly focused on the current and potential customers surrounding us. We must also maintain a keen awareness of those individuals who support our efforts daily. They can be found everywhere within our organizational structure. We must nurture these internal partnerships and treat them as equal partners in our success.

Nothing happens until something is sold. This cliché was true yesterday; its true today and it will be true tomorrow. Therefore, as sales professionals, the true success of our business rides on our shoulders. We are placed front and center with all eyes on us, and this position requires us to be smart, strong, creative and true leaders within our organization. We wrote this book for you. We realize how important it is for you to be wildly successful and we are confident that you will achieve much by living the principles we have discussed and following the processes we have outlined. We look forward to developing a strong and lasting relationship with you. For more free tools to support your efforts and additional information on our online and live seminar courses, please feel free to visit www.salesuniverse.com. You are a high earning, highly successful, salesperson and a representative of an honorable profession. Believe it, live it, enjoy it and be grateful for it.

Bibliography

1. Alda Stephens, , Discover, The Outtop, 50 memorable quotes by John Maxwell, July, 2014 <https://theouttop.com/50-inspirational-john-maxwell-quotes-on-leadership-productivity/>
2. Goodreads, Quotes: http://www.goodreads.com/quotes/296303-when-you-are-able-to-shift-your-inner-awareness-to
3. Quote Sigma, 69 Memorable Quotes by Ernest Hemingway, files. 2015 <http://www.quotesigma.com/69-memorable-quotes-by-ernest-hemingway/>
4. Brainy Quote, desktop , 2 copyright 2001-2015 <http://www.brainyquote.com/quotes/quotes/a/abrahamlin151229.html>
5. Garrison Keeler, The Writer's Almanac, 2005 <http://writersalmanac.publicradio.org/index.php?date=2005/02/01>
6. Wikipedia, the Law of Attraction, August 20, 2015 <https://en.wikipedia.org/wiki/Law_of_attraction_(New_Thought)>

7. Dale Carnegie Training, the Carnegie principles, 2008 <http://www.dcarnegietraining.com/resources/relationship-principles>
8. Stephen R. Covey, *The 7 Habits of Highly Effective People*, Kingsway, London, Simon & Schuster, copyright 2001
9. James Allen, *As A Man Thinketh*, Golgotha press, 2011
10. Michael Moncur, The Quotations Page, 2015, <http://www.quotationspage.com/quote/9316.html>
11. Goodreads, David Allen quotes, <http://www.goodreads.com/quotes/575493>
12. Praise for Loyalty Myths by Keiningham, Vavra, Aksoy, and Wallard <http://www.ipsos.com/loyalty/sites/ipsos.com.loyalty/files/Ipsos_Loyalty_Myth_8_Excerpt_0.pdf>
13. W. Edwards Deming, *Out of the Crisis*, The MIT Press; Reprint edition (August 11, 2000)
14. David H. Maister, Charles H. Green, Robert M. Galford, *The Trusted Advisor*, Free Press (October 9, 2001)
15. Addicted to Success, addicted2success.com, 2015 <http://addicted2success.com/quotes/50-powerful-tony-robbins-quotes-that-has-changed-my-life/>
16. John C. Maxwell, *Developing the Leader Within You*, Thomas Nelson; 1 edition (October 2, 2005)
17. Benjamin Franklin, *Poor Richard's Almanac*, Skyhorse Publishing, Inc., Dec 13, 2013

www.ingramcontent.com/pod-product-compliance
Lightning Source LLC
Jackson TN
JSHW080202141224
75386JS00029B/999
* 9 7 8 1 6 3 0 4 7 8 2 9 2 *